So you really want to lea

Spanish

BOOK 2

So you really want to learn

Spanish

BOOK 2

Simon Craft M.A. (Oxon.), PGCE (Bristol)
Series Editor: Nicholas Oulton M.A. (Oxon.)

GALORE PARK

Published by Galore Park Publishing Ltd,
PO Box 96, Cranbrook, Kent TN17 4WS

Text copyright © Simon Craft 2004
Illustrations copyright © Galore Park 2004
Printed and bound by The Bath Press

ISBN 1 902984 26 9

First published 2004

Available in the series:

So you really want to learn Spanish Book 1
    Pupil's Book   1902984102
    Teacher's book   1902984137
    Audio CD set   1902984250

So you really want to learn Spanish Book 2
    Pupil's Book   1902984269
    Teacher's book   1902984277
    Audio CD set   1902984285

So you really want to learn Spanish Book 3
    Pupil's Book   1902984307
    Teacher's book   1902984390
    Audio CD set   1902984404

Acknowledgements

The author and publisher would like to thank the following for permission to use copyright material:
'El País'
Karlos Arguiñano

We would also like to thank the following for their contributions: Professor Rafael Fente (University of Granada), Mari-Ángeles Márquez (Lectora, Westminster School), John Witney (Westminster School), Cinta Romero (Bethany School) and, *especialmente*, **Miguel Márquez ('Mique')**. Thanks also to Florence Buet, for her splendid ferrying duties and Ian Douglass for the fabulous pictures.

Preface

Welcome to 'So you really want to learn Spanish' Book 2, in which we have striven to combine an entertaining and amusing narrative style with a comprehensive grammatical approach. In this way, we hope that you will continue to master the language and enjoy yourselves at the same time. In this book, and indeed Book 3, you will follow the trials and tribulations of the magnificent Jorge and other endearing characters, who will appear regularly throughout the units. ¡Que lo paséis bien!

Contents

Unit 1 – Nos presentamos

Unit 2 – La comida

Unit 3 – La salud

Unit 4 – De compras

Unit 5 – El turismo

Unit 6 – Diversiones

Glosarios

About the unit

In this first unit you will learn to describe, comprehend and compare personal characteristics. You will learn how to make simple introductions and to express thanks and appreciation.

New language content:

- use of *poco* as both an adjective and adverb
- comparative and superlative adjectives
- formation of adverbs
- direct object pronouns e.g. *lo, la, los, las*

New contexts:

- character descriptions
- meeting people, formally and informally
- being and welcoming a guest
- expressing thanks in speech and in an informal letter

Me presento

You are going to begin this second book by learning to describe yourself, in terms of your personal characteristics and your likes and dislikes. As far as personal descriptions are concerned, you will need to remember to use the verb *ser*, as you will be referring to characteristics that are not changeable, e.g. *soy alto y delgado*. You will also need to remember to use *tener* with certain physical descriptions, e.g. *tengo los ojos azules*.

Exercise 1.1 👂 ✍ 🗨

¡Escucha, toma apuntes y luego habla!

Listen to the person describing himself and take notes (*apuntes*) of what he says. Suggested headings for your notes are given below. Be prepared to answer the questions below.

> **Apuntes:**
> Nombre:
> Edad:
> Familia:
> Pasatiempos:
> Físico:

1. *¿Cómo se llama?* . . . .
2. *¿Cuántos años tiene?* . . . .
3. *¿Qué información hay sobre sus padres?* . . . .
4. *¿Cómo se lleva con su hermana y por qué?* . . . . . .
5. *¿Qué le gusta?* . . . .
6. *¿Cómo es físicamente?* . . . .

> **Vocabulario**
> *¡Toma apuntes!* = take notes!
> *Andaluz* = from the region of *Andalucía*
> *A causa de* = because of
> *El abogado* = the lawyer
> *Llevarse fatal* = to get on very badly
> *Un montón de* = loads of
> *Puesto que* = because, since
> *El sentido* = the sense

Exercise 1.2 ✍

¡Escribe!

Now write a short description of yourself using the format used by Pepe. Try to incorporate some of the adjectives from the list below. Obviously, don't feel obliged to use the words *feo* and *antipático*!

> **Vocabulario**
> *Deportivo* = sporty
> *Antipático* = not so nice!
> *Guapo* = good-looking
> *Tranquilo* = calm
> *Perezoso* = lazy
> *Simpático* = nice, kind
> *Generoso* = generous
> *Feo* = ugly
> *Extrovertido* = extrovert
> *Feliz* = happy, good-natured

Exercise 1.3

¡Escribe!

It is very important when both writing and speaking Spanish that you try to remember to make agreements.

1. Check that you have made the verb agree with its subject, e.g. *el hombre <u>es</u> gordo y feo*.
2. Check that the adjectives agree with the nouns they describe. For example, if Pepe wanted to be rude about Yolanda (who is feminine), he would say *mi hermana es <u>gorda</u> y <u>fea</u>*. Remember, of course, that adjectives that end in *e* do not change in the feminine (see Book 1, page 39). Also, with few exceptions (such as nationalities), adjectives that end in consonants do not tend to change, e.g *un libro azul, una mesa azul*.

Well, now we've sorted that one out, let's try to put it into practice. You need to fill in the gaps in the sentences below, inserting the correct form of both the verb and the adjective in brackets.

1. *Mi suegra (SER) (GUAPO)*
2. *Su nieto (TENER) los ojos (AZUL)*
3. *Sus hijas (SER) (INTELIGENTE)*
4. *Yo (TENER) una camisa (NEGRO)*
5. *Nosotros (ESTAR) (CANSADO)*

> **Vocabulario**
> *La suegra* = mother-in-law
> *La camisa* = the shirt
> *Cansado* = tired

Exercise 1.4

CD1: 2

¡Lee y escucha!
Lee o escucha esta conversación y luego contesta las preguntas.

Ramón:	*Hola. Yo me llamo Ramón, ¿y tú ?*
Paco:	*Yo soy Francisco, pero todo el mundo me llama Paco. Encantado de conocerte.*
Ramón:	*Igualmente. ¿Tienes muchos hermanos?*
Paco:	*Bueno, tengo dos hermanos y una hermana. ¿Y tú ?*
Ramón:	*Yo tengo una hermana.*
Paco:	*¿Te llevas bien con ella?*
Ramón:	*Sí, porque siempre me presenta a todas sus amigas guapas.*
Paco:	*¡Qué suerte! Yo me llevo fatal con la mía. Es muy antipática.*
Ramón:	*¿Por qué?*
Paco:	*Porque nunca me deja ver el fútbol. Es que es mayor que yo y siempre quiere ver 'Operación Triunfo'.*
Ramón:	*¿Qué es eso ?*
Paco:	*¿Realmente no lo sabes? Es un programa de música.*
Ramón:	*Es que nosotros no tenemos televisión en casa.*
Paco:	*¡Qué raro! De todas formas me gustaría ir a tu casa. Tu hermana parece ser mucho más simpática que la mía.*
Ramón:	*Bueno. Puedes venir esta noche si quieres.*
Paco:	*¡Estupendo!*

> **Vocabulario**
> *Encantado de conocerte* = pleased to meet you
> *Igualmente* = same here
> *Llevarse bien/fatal con* = to get on well/badly with
> *Mayor* = older
> *Dejar* = to allow
> *¡Qué raro!* = How strange!
> *De todas formas* = anyhow
> *Me gustaría* = I would like
> *Parecer* = to seem, appear
> *Estupendo* = fantastic

Contesta estas preguntas:

1.   *¿Quién tiene la familia más numerosa, Ramón o Paco?*
2.   *¿Quién dice que su hermana es más simpática, Ramón o Paco, y por qué?*
3.   *¿Por qué Paco no puede ver el fútbol?*
4.   *¿Cuándo va Paco a casa de Ramón?*

Notice how the conversation has been conducted using the 2nd person *tú* form rather than the 3rd person *usted* form. Although the *usted* mode of address is still a very important one in Spain, it is not quite as widely used as it used to be. It certainly would not be appropriate for two young people meeting one another for the first time.

Comparative and superlative adjectives

Adjectives may be *compared* in three degrees: positive, comparative and superlative. The **positive** is the adjective in its normal state; the **comparative** is used to say 'more', and the **superlative** is used to say 'very' or 'most'.

An example of the **comparative** would be Paco **is uglier (or more ugly) than** Yolanda. In other words, you are making a comparison between one thing (in this case a person) and another. An example of the **superlative** would be, at the risk of insulting Paco once again, **he is the ugliest (or most ugly) person in Andalucía.** As you can see, in this case, we are stating an absolute extreme.

1.   In Spanish, as you will have noticed earlier in the unit, the **comparative** is formed by using the following:

Más .... que or **menos ....que**, inserting the appropriate adjective in the gap.
E.g.   *Mi hermano es **más delgado que** yo* = my brother is **thinner** than me.

E.g.   *Yo soy **menos delgado que** mi hermano* = I am **less thin** than my brother.

2.   The **superlative** is formed by using **más/menos** without **que** followed by the adjective concerned after the noun.

E.g.   *Es la chica **más guapa** de la clase* = she is **the prettiest** girl in the class.

E.g.   *Es el chico **menos inteligente** del colegio* = he is **the least intelligent** boy in the school.

Sadly, as ever, there are some exceptions. Here they are:

Positive	Comparative	Superlative
Bueno	*mejor que*	*mejor*
Malo	*peor que*	*peor*
Viejo	*mayor que*	*mayor*
Joven	*menor que*	*menor*

Es la chica más guapa de la clase

Exercise 1.5

¡Escribe!
Inventa algunas frases como las de los ejemplos.

Using some of the adjectives and nouns used so far in the unit, invent three sentences using the comparative **más/menos que** and then three using the superlative **más/menos**.

E.g.   *Paco es más guapo que Pepe.*

E.g.   *Pepe es el chico más feo del colegio.*

Exercise 1.6

¡Escucha!
Escucha la conversación y contesta las preguntas.

1.   *¿De qué nacionalidad son Elena y Angela?*
2.   *¿Por qué Angela prefiere Granada?*
3.   *¿Por qué dice Angela que Granada no es perfecta?*
4.   *¿Por qué está extrañada Elena?*

Exercise 1.7

¡Escribe!
Mira los dibujos de abajo y compara a las distintas personas.
Escribe 8 frases diferentes como en el ejemplo.

E.g.   *Juanjo es mucho más alto que Antonio. También es más guapo.*

> **Vocabulario**
> *Relajado* = relaxed
> *Además* = besides
> *Sucio* = dirty
> *El sitio* = place
> *Seguro* = safe
> *Tan* = so
> *Ninguno* (*ningún* before masculine
>   singular noun) = no
> *Extrañar* = to surprise
> *Ruidoso* = noisy
> *El planeta* = the planet
> *¡Qué va!* = No way!

Luisa   Juanjo   Jorge   Manuela   Antonio

CD1:
4

Exercise 1.8

¡Lee y escribe!
Lee esta conversación y coloca estas palabras en el sitio correcto.

diez	muy	es	estoy
mayor	egoísta	siento	más cansado
mundo	más	generoso	

Paco: Oye, Julio, ¿por qué no compras el pan hoy?
Julio: Pero tú has dormido mucho más que yo, y yo......... mucho .... que tú.
Paco: Mira, yo soy .... que tú, y tienes que obedecerme.
Julio: Pero eso es .... injusto. Eres un ....
Paco: Lo .... El..............es así.
Julio: Y otra cosa. Me debes .... euros.
Paco: Si eres .... que yo, ése no ... mi problema.

Vocabulario
Colocar = to place
Has dormido = you have slept
Obedecer = to obey
Egoísta = selfish
Mundo = world
Injusto = unfair

Exercise 1.9

¡Escribe!
Study the dialogue in Exercise 1.8. Then, using the adjectives below, compare Paco and Julio.

Egoísta
Mayor
Generoso
Menor

1. Paco es.................................Julio.
2. Paco es.................................Julio.
3. Julio es.................................Paco.
4. Julio es.................................Paco.

Una carta

We are now going to learn how to compose an informal letter in Spanish. This task is often required at examination level, but you may well find that there are occasions in real life when this will prove useful. When addressing the person concerned at the beginning, you will need to use the appropriate form of *querido*, e.g. *Querido Juan/Querida Juana*, followed by a colon. For the ending, you could use *Un abrazo* (Love from) or *Recuerdos* (Regards).

Exercise 1.10

¡Lee!

Lee esta carta y luego escribe una respuesta, contestando las preguntas que te hace Julia.

> *Londres, 18 de mayo*
>
> *Querida María:*
>
> *Hola, ¿qué tal? Yo me llamo Julia. Soy inglesa, tengo quince años, y soy la hija de unos amigos de tus padres. Resulta que me interesa mucho la idea de hacer un intercambio con un chico o una chica de mi edad. A ver si describo cómo soy y lo que me gusta y no me gusta, y luego podemos ver si tenemos los mismos gustos o no. Soy bastante alta con el pelo rubio y los ojos azules. ¿Cómo eres tú? Vivo con mis padres y mi hermano, Richard, en una casa bastante grande en las afueras de Londres. ¿Dónde vives tú y qué te parece? ¿Cómo te llevas con tu familia? Yo me llevo muy bien con mis padres porque son muy tolerantes, pero me llevo fatal con Richard. Es mucho más inteligente que yo, pero bastante más antipático. Si tienes hermanos, ¿cómo son? A mí, me encanta ir al cine y salir con mis amigos los fines de semana. No soy muy deportista pero me gusta esquiar. Me gusta muchísimo viajar, y mi país favorito es España que conozco mucho porque mi madre es de Sevilla. Estoy loca por las telenovelas en la televisión. Me gusta mucho comprar ropa y música, pero no me gusta tener que ir al supermercado con mi madre para hacer la compra. Tampoco me gusta tener que ir de vacaciones con mi hermano. ¡Qué horror! Cuéntame lo que te gusta hacer a ti y, también, lo que no te gusta. ¿Cuál es tu país favorito?*
>
> *Bueno, tengo muchas ganas de conocerte mejor. A ver si me contestas pronto.*
>
> *Un abrazo muy fuerte.*
>
> *Julia*

Ahora, escribe una carta a Julia que incluya una respuesta a todas sus preguntas. Usa aproximadamente 120 palabras.

> **Vocabulario**
> *Resulta* = the fact is/it transpires
> *Interesar* = to interest
> *Un intercambio* = an exchange
> *A ver si* = let's see whether, let's hope that
> *Los gustos* = tastes/interests
> *Las afueras* = the outskirts
> *¿Qué te parece?* = what do you think about it?
> *Muchísimo* = very much
> *Estar loco por* = to be crazy about
> *Hacer la compra* = to do the shopping
> *Tampoco* = neither
> *Cuéntame* = tell me (*contar* = to tell/relate)
> *La gana* = the wish, desire

Exercise 1.11

¡Escucha y toma apuntes!

Apuntes:

	Carlos	María	Jorge
Dónde vive:	. . . .	. . . .	. . . .
Físico:	. . . .	. . . .	. . . .
Familia:	. . . .	. . . .	. . . .
Pasatiempos:	. . . .	. . . .	. . . .
Colegio:	. . . .	. . . .	. . . .
Viajes:	. . . .	. . . .	. . . .
Otros:	. . . .	. . . .	. . . .

Vocabulario

Echar de menos = to miss
Medir (i) = to be of a certain height
Regañar = to tell off
Entenderse bien = to get on well
La película = the film
Extranjero = foreign
Demasiado = too much
Entretenido = entertaining
Sino = but also
Liso = straight (hair)
Yo no sé = I don't know
Marchosa = extrovert
El novio = the boyfriend
Gastar = to spend (money)

El dinero = the money
He viajado = I have travelled
Sería = it would be
Verdadero = true, real
Las "chuches" = the sweets
La afición = the pastime, hobby
El toreo = bullfighting
Coche = car
En cuanto = as soon as
Sacarse el carné = to get one's driving licence
Tengo muchas ganas = I really want
La sidra = the cider
Escaparse = to escape, get away

Exercise 1.12

¡Escribe!
¿Tú a quién prefieres?

Using what you have learnt about Carlos, María and El Gordo, state which of the three people you prefer, and which one you like least, giving reasons for your choice in each case. Use the notes and vocabulary you took previously. You should aim to write approximately 40 – 50 words for each one.

Verbs like gustar

You will have noticed when listening to Carlos, Jorge and María that verbs such as *gustar* and *encantar* are very useful when describing likes and dislikes, hobbies and pastimes. Indeed, you will know by now that there are many other verbs in Spanish that work in exactly the same way and which are not confined to describing people's interests. You will recall that these verbs do not function like normal ones. Just to remind you, if, for example, you want to say 'I like hamburguers', you have to say 'hamburguers are pleasing to me', i.e. '*me gustan las hamburguesas.'* Notice that the subject *(las hamburguesas)* comes **after** the verb here. This is a common feature of the use of this type of verb. You will find that these verbs are usually used in their 3rd person forms, both singular and plural. Other common verbs of this kind are *parecer* (to seem, appear), *importar* (to mind) and, in particular, *doler* (to ache, hurt), which we will deal with at some length in Unit 3.

CD1: 5-7

Exercise 1.13

¡Escucha!
Escucha a Carlos, María y Jorge otra vez, y apunta abajo todos los ejemplos posibles del uso de **gustar** y **encantar**.

1. Carlos
2. María
3. Jorge

Exercise 1.14

¡Escribe!
Traduce estas frases al español:

1. I like going out with my friends.
2. He loves eating.
3. She likes skiing and travelling.
4. Do you (singular) like hamburguers?
5. He likes sports.

*Ahora, inventa 5 frases diferentes con **gustar** y **encantar.** A ver si puedes usar formas diferentes de cada verbo.*

Los adverbios

Adverbs in English often end in **–ly**, e.g. **slowly, sadly, normally, reasonably.** These words are used to qualify a verb, e.g. **he ran slowly.** The verb in this case is obviously **'ran'** and the adverb which qualifies it is **'slowly'.** You can see the connection between the adjective **slow** and the adverb **slowly.** The **–ly** ending tells you that it's an adverb. There is a very strong parallel in Spanish. To form the adverb in Spanish, you take the **FEMININE** form of the adjective and add –*mente* to this. Study the examples below:

Adjective	**Feminine**	**Adverb**	
Lento	*lenta*	*lentamente*	= slowly
Alegre	*alegre*	*alegremente*	= happily
Hábil	*hábil*	*hábilmente*	= skilfully

Vocabulario 1.1

As in Book 1, in this book we will be giving you regular vocabularies to learn, normaly at the rate of two per unit. Here is the first one!

Vocabulario 1.1

A causa de = because of
Además = besides
La afición = the pastime, hobby
El apunte = the note
La camisa = the shirt
Cansado = tired
Las "chuches" (chucherías) = sweets
Contar = to tell
Dejar = to allow, let
Demasiado = too much
Deportivo = sporty
De todas formas = at any rate, anyhow
Egoísta = selfish
En cuanto = as soon as
Encantado = pleased (to meet you)
Entenderse = to get on with
Entretenido = entertaining
Escaparse = to escape, get away
Esquiar = to ski
Estupendo = fantastic, wonderful
Extranjero = foreign
Extrañar = to surprise
Extrovertido = outgoing
Feliz = happy
Feo = ugly
La gana = the wish, desire
Gastar = to spend (money)
Generoso = generous
Hábil = skilful
Hacer la compra = to do the shopping
Igualmente = likewise

Injusto = unfair
Interesar = to interest
Lento = slow
Liso = straight (hair)
Loco = crazy
Luego = then
Marchoso = extrovert
Mayor = older
Medir = to be of a certain height
(Un) montón de = loads of, piles of
El mundo = the world
El novio = the boyfriend
Obedecer = to obey
Parecer = to seem, appear
La película = the film
El programa = programme
Puesto que = since, because
Rápido = quick, quickly
Raro = strange, odd
Regañar = to tell off
Ruidoso = noisy
El sentido = the sense
El sitio = the place
Sucio = dirty
La suegra = the mother-in-law
Tampoco = neither
La telenovela = the soap opera
Tranquilo = calm
Triste = sad
Verdadero = true, real
Viajar = to travel

Exercise 1.15

¡Escribe!
Mira esta lista de adjetivos y a ver si puedes escribir el adverbio.

E.g.   *alegre* becomes *alegremente*

Los adjetivos:

1.   *rápido*
2.   *lento*
3.   *loco*
4.   *triste*
5.   *feliz*

Exercise 1.16

¡Escribe!
Usando los 5 adverbios de Exercise 1.15, escribe 5 frases completas abajo.

E.g. *Jorge come la hamburguesa rápidamente.*

CD2:
8

Exercise 1.17

¡Lee!
Lee este texto y luego pon el adverbio correcto en su sitio.

Julio está muy enfadado con su hermano y sale de su dormitorio ....Pero ya son las nueve y media y ....desayunan a las nueve. Tiene mucha prisa y entonces va......................a la panadería. Pero el panadero ya es muy viejo y trabaja bastante......................Ya es tarde. Julio mira su reloj......................Sus padres van a estar muy enfadados. ....le atiende el panadero. Cuando llega Julio a casa, son las diez y cuarto. '¿Dónde demonios has estado?' le pregunta......................su padre.

Los adverbios:
Rápidamente   Normalmente
Lentamente   Nerviosamente
Furiosamente (x 2)   Finalmente

Vocabulario
Enfadado = angry
Tener prisa = to be in a hurry
El panadero = the baker
Atender = to serve
¿Dónde demonios has estado? = Where on earth have you been?

Exercise 1.18

¡Escribe!
Trabajo creativo

Elige tres de los adverbios de arriba y tres de las palabras en la lista de vocabulario. Luego inventa una pequeña historia de unas 70 palabras. Obviamente, tienes que añadir muchas otras palabras.

Ouch – direct object pronouns

Direct object pronouns sound nasty, but their bark is a lot worse than their bite. They are simply words such as **me, you, him, us** which we use in place of a noun. Let's consider a sentence such as 'Jorge is eating the sandwich'. The direct object in this case is 'the sandwich'. The appropriate pronoun in English is 'it', i.e. 'Jorge is eating it'.

Now let's look at this in Spanish:

Jorge come el bocadillo = Jorge eats the sandwich.

If we replace the noun, *el bocadillo* with a pronoun, the sentence would be:

Jorge lo come = Jorge eats it.

So here are the direct object pronouns:

Singular			Plural		
Me	=	me	*nos*	=	us
Te	=	you (singular)	*os*	=	you (plural)
Lo	=	him/it (masculine)	*los*	=	them (masculine)
La	=	her/it (feminine)	*las*	=	them (feminine)

N.B. There is another pronoun *le* which can be used as an alternative for 'him'. Both *le* and *lo* are used. Also, the pronouns *lo, la, los* and *las* can also mean 'you' when they stand for *usted* in the polite form.

Location, location, location

Now that we've learnt our direct object pronouns, here are a few words of advice about where to put them:

1. When you use a verb in a tense, as in the example with *Jorge* above, the pronoun must go before the verb.

E.g. *Jorge **lo** come* = Jorge is eating it.

2. If the verb is a positive imperative, the direct object pronoun must be added to the end of the imperative.

E.g. *¡Cómelo!* = eat it!

3.   If the verb is followed by the infinitive or gerund, the direct object pronoun either goes before the main verb or on the end of the infinitive or participle. **It cannot go in the middle.** Study these examples:

E.g.   *Jorge **lo** está comiendo = Jorge* is eating it.

E.g.   *Jorge está comiéndo**lo** = Jorge* is eating it.

E.g.   *Jorge **lo** va a comer = Jorge* is going to eat it.

E.g.   *Jorge va a comer**lo** = Jorge* is going to eat it.

Exercise 1.19

¡Lee!

Lee este diálogo entre Carlos, Manolo y su madre, y luego haz una lista de todos los ejemplos del uso del pronombre.

Carlos:	*Esta noche ponen el partido entre el Betis y el Sevilla. ¿Te apetece verlo?*
Manolo:	*¿A qué hora lo ponen?*
Carlos:	*A las nueve.*
Madre:	*Lo siento. Tenemos que ir a casa de la abuela.*
Carlos:	*Pero mamá, ¿otra vez?*
Madre:	*¿Es que no queréis verla?*
Manolo:	*Claro que queremos verla, pero la vamos a ver el domingo también.*
Madre:	*¿Y los deberes, los habéis hecho?*
Manolo:	*Yo no tengo.*
Carlos:	*Voy a hacerlos ahora mismo.*
Madre:	*Bueno, pero quita la tele.*
Carlos:	*Pero mamá, quiero ver 'El rival más débil'.*
Madre:	*Quítala te digo.*
Carlos:	*Vale, vale.*

> **Vocabulario**
> *El partido* = the match
> *Apetecer* = to feel like/want
> *¿Los habéis hecho?* = have you done them?
> *'El rival más débil'* = 'the weakest link'
> *Quitar* = to switch off

Exercise 1.20

¡Escribe!

Escribe estas frases otra vez, sustituyendo los sustantivos con el pronombre correcto.

Notice that when we use the direct object pronoun rather than the noun, the personal 'a' disappears.

E.g.   *Veo a Ramón* = I see Ramón.

     Lo veo = I see him.

1.   *Está comiendo las galletas.*
2.   *¡Come la naranja!*
3.   *Quiero ver el partido.*
4.   *Vamos a ver a mi tía, mañana.*
5.   *Ven a sus profesores.*

Exercise 1.21

¡Escribe!
Ahora inventa 5 frases como las de arriba, y luego, debajo, sustituye el pronombre por el sustantivo.

Ejemplos:
Carlos no quiere hacer los deberes = Carlos no quiere hacerlos.
Jorge está viendo el partido = Jorge lo está viendo.

Exercise 1.22

¡Lee y escribe!
*Lee esta carta y haz una lista debajo de todos los ejemplos de los pronombres **lo, la, los, las.** También, haz una lista de los adverbios.*

> *Granada, 3 de marzo de 2003*
>
> *Querida Julia:*
>
> *Muchas gracias por tu carta. La recibí ayer. ¡Qué ilusión! Obviamente, tenemos muchas cosas en común. La idea de hacer un intercambio me interesa mucho. A mí también me gustan las telenovelas. Normalmente las veo todos los días. ¿Cómo son las telenovelas allí? ¿Cuándo las ves? ¿También te gusta la música? ¿Conoces a Miguel Bosé? Si no, te lo voy a poner cuando vengas. Tengo todos sus discos.*
>
> *Voy a hablar con mis padres sobre el intercambio. Yo creo que es una idea fantástica. Granada te va a gustar, sobre todo si te gusta esquiar. Si vienes en abril, podemos subir a la sierra y luego, si hace bueno, ir a la playa. Generalmente, yo voy todos los fines de semana. ¿Qué haces normalmente los fines de semana en Londres?*
>
> *Bueno, tengo que irme porque el culebrón está a punto de empezar.*
>
> *Escríbeme pronto.*
>
> *Un abrazo.*
>
> *María*

Exercise 1.23

¡Escribe!
Ahora, escribe una respuesta a María. Trata de contestar sus preguntas. También, trata de usar algunos pronombres y adverbios. Trata de usar entre 100 y 120 palabras.

Vocabulario
Recibí = I received (*recibir* = to receive)
¡Qué ilusión! = How exciting!
El culebrón = the soap opera
Estar a punto de = to be about to
Cuando vengas = when you come
La sierra = the mountain
Tratar de = to try to

Revision: The future

You will have seen from the letter that María says she **is going to** speak to her parents. The way she does this is by using the verb *ir* followed by the preposition *a* and then the infinitive. This is a largely failsafe way of describing future plans, events etc. Well, it is failsafe as long as you can remember how the verb *ir* works in the present tense. Let's see if you can complete the following sentences correctly.

Exercise 1.24

¡Escribe!
Completa las frases de abajo, usando la forma correcta de **ir** *y añadiendo un infinitivo de esta lista.*

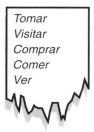

Tomar
Visitar
Comprar
Comer
Ver

Ejemplo:
Julio ... a .... a su hermano.
Julio **va** *a* **visitar** *a su hermano* = *Julio* is going to visit his brother.

1.　　Yo .... a.................pan con el dinero.
2.　　Mis padres.................a ....a mi abuela.
3.　　¿Tú ....a.................la película?
4.　　Jorge ....a ....cinco bocadillos enormes.
5.　　Nosotros ....a ....una cerveza.

Exercise 1.25

¡Escribe!
Inventa 5 frases usando **ir,** *la preposición* **a** *y un* **infinitivo**.

Ejemplo:
Voy a escribir *5 frases.*

CD1:
10

Exercise 1.26

¡Escucha!
Escucha esta conversación entre Julia, María, y la madre de María, y contesta las preguntas.

1.　　¿Qué dice Julia de su viaje y por qué?
2.　　¿Qué significa la palabra **embutidos**?
3.　　¿Qué le apetece comer a Julia?
4.　　¿Qué quiere comer María?
5.　　¿Qué quieren beber?

Exercise 1.27

¡Escribe y habla!

Role-play. Working in pairs, invent your own conversation between an English pupil and the mother or father of your Spanish exchange partner. The situation is the same as that in Exercise 1.26, i.e. you have just arrived at your exchange partner's house in Spain. Each person should have at least 5 lines. Try to incorporate your own comments about food and drink.

Exercise 1.28

¡Lee!

Lee esta conversación entre María y Julia y luego contesta las preguntas.

María: Bueno, Julia, ¿qué tal tu habitación, te gusta?

Julia: Sí, está muy bien. Es mucho más grande que mi cuarto en Londres. Mira, te traigo un regalo.

María: Muchísimas gracias. ¿Qué es?

Julia: Como te gusta la música, aquí tienes un CD de "The Stone Roses".

María: ¿Las rosas de piedra?

Julia: Sí, así es.

María: Un nombre interesante. Muchas gracias. Yo también tengo un regalo para ti. Toma.

Julia: Un CD de 'Operación Triunfo'. ¡Qué maravilla! Muchas gracias.

María: De nada. ¿Qué te apetece hacer luego?

Julia: No sé. Lo que quieras.

María: ¿Qué tal si salimos de tapas? ¿Te gusta tapear?

Julia: Sí, mucho. Suena muy bien.

> **Vocabulario**
> *La habitación* = the room, bedroom
> *El cuarto* = the room, bedroom
> *Traer* = to bring (*traigo* = I have brought)
> *Un regalo* = a present
> *Lo que quieras* = whatever you like
> *Salir de tapas* = to go out and eat tapas
> *Tapear* = to eat tapas
> *Suena muy bien* = that sounds really good

Contesta estas preguntas:

1. ¿Qué dice Julia de su habitación en Granada?
2. ¿Cuál es el regalo de María para Julia?
3. ¿Qué van a hacer luego?

Exercise 1.29

¡Escribe!

Role-play. Working in pairs, invent a dialogue in Spanish between Jorge and his English exchange partner. The format should be the same as that between Julia and María, i.e. you have just been shown your room and are exchanging gifts. It would, of course, be no surprise if these were related to food in some shape or form. Each person should have six lines.

Formal and informal

You will now be familiar with the *usted* form in Spanish and will know that it is still a vital part of the language. However, it is true to say that we all live in a more informal society in this day and age, and that, as such, the *usted* form is not as widely-used as it was. You will have seen an example of this in Exercise 1.26 when the mother of María tells Julia not to worry about addressing her in the *usted* form. This is not to underestimate in any way the huge significance of *usted*, simply to point out that it is not used as much now in certain contexts.

It is all a question of establishing the correct 'register'. For example, if the mother of María was very formal and a little old-fashioned, she might well have expected Julia to have addressed her as *usted*. In this event, if Julia were to have written a thank-you letter, she would have used this more formal mode of address. However, because the mother is obviously modern in terms of her outlook, coupled with the fact that she welcomes Julia as part of the family, it would be more natural for a thank-you letter to be written using a more informal tone.

Let's now consider how both a formal and informal letter begin and end.

FORMAL: One can begin with either *Muy señor mío* or *Estimado señor* or their appropriate variations, i.e. *Muy señora mía* or *Estimados señores*. A standard ending would be *Le saluda atentamente* followed by a signature.

INFORMAL: As we have seen, one should begin with the appropriate form of the adjective *querido*, e.g. *Querida María/Queridos primos* etc. An appropriate ending would be *Un abrazo* or *Recuerdos*.

Another factor to bear in mind is that whilst one would clearly use either the *tú* or *vosotros* form when writing an informal letter, the 3rd person *usted/ustedes* would be required in a formal letter. Consider the following examples:

FORMAL:
Estimada señora:
Gracias por **su** *carta.*

INFORMAL:
Querido Paco:
Gracias por **tu** *carta.*

N.B. If you were writing an informal letter addressed to more that one person, as in the case of the next exercise, *tu* would be replaced by the correct form of *vuestro*.

E.g.   *En vuestra casa* = in your house (i.e. the house where you [plural] live).

Exercise 1.30 📖 ✍️ 💬

¡Lee!
Lee esta carta de Julia a la familia de María y luego contesta las preguntas.

Londres, 3 de mayo

Querida familia Márquez:

Os escribo para daros las gracias por una estancia realmente maravillosa en vuestra casa. Lo pasé bomba. Muchas gracias por vuestra generosidad y por enseñarme tantos sitios preciosos. Me encantan todos esos bares de tapas, sobre todo 'La Papa' donde ponen todos esos platos diferentes de patatas. También me gustó mucho ese bar cerca de Plaza Nueva donde ponen ese pescado tan bueno. ¡Qué gambas más ricas!

Gracias, también, por llevarme a La Alhambra. Es un sitio verdaderamente impresionante. Los jardines son especialmente bonitos con tanta agua y tantas flores. ¡Qué maravilla!

María, muchas gracias por el regalo. Me encanta. Mi familia se está volviendo loca porque pongo el disco de 'Operación Triunfo' todos los días. Creo que ya están un poco hartos de David Bisbal.

Los embutidos también son un éxito. Nos hemos comido casi todo el jamón y el queso. Se vende esa comida aquí, pero es mucho más cara que en España. Mi padre también os da las gracias. Ya se ha bebido las cinco botellas de vino tinto. Hemos tenido que comprar más aspirinas como consecuencia de eso. A mi madre le encanta el perfume.

Bueno, tengo que irme porque 'Neighbours' empieza dentro de cinco minutos y quiero sentarme en el mejor sillón antes que mi hermano.

Un abrazo muy, muy fuerte, y otra vez, muchísimas gracias por todo.

Julia

Vocabulario

Una estancia = a stay	*Volverse loco* = to go crazy
Lo pasé bomba = I had a fantastic time	*Poner el disco* = to play the record
Enseñar = to show	*Estar harto* = to be fed up
Un bar de tapas = a *tapas* bar	*Nos hemos comido* = we've eaten
Me gustó = I liked	*Se ha bebido* = he has drunk
El pescado = fish (food)	*Hemos tenido que* = we have had to
Estar bueno = to be tasty	*Ser un éxito* = to be a success
La gamba = the prawn	*Como consecuencia* = as a result
Rico = tasty	*El vino tinto* = red wine
Verdaderamente = really	*Dentro de 5 minutos* = in 5 minutes' time
	El sillón = the armchair

Contesta estas preguntas:

1. *¿Por qué a Julia le gusta tanto 'La Papa'?*
2. *¿Por qué le gustó el bar cerca de Plaza Nueva?*
3. *¿Qué dice de La Alhambra y por qué le gusta tanto?*
4. *¿Qué piensa la familia de Julia de David Bisbal y por qué?*
5. *¿Por qué es mejor comprar embutidos en España?*
6. *¿Cuántas de las 5 botellas de vino quedan?*
7. *¿Qué regalo tiene la madre de Julia?*
8. *¿Por qué tiene prisa Julia?*

Vocabulario
Tener prisa = to be in a hurry
Quedar = to remain/to be left over
Le gustó = she liked

Exercise 1.31

¡Escribe!
Ahora, usando la carta de Julia como un ejemplo, escribe una carta a la familia de Jorge, dándole las gracias por tu estancia. Usa unas 120 palabras.

Vocabulario 1.2

And here is your second vocabulary for this unit.

Vocabulario 1.2

Apetecer = to feel like	*El partido* = the match
El bocadillo = the sandwich	*El pescado* = fish
El cuarto = the room, bedroom	*Poner el disco* = to play a record
Dentro de 5 minutos = in 5 minutes' time	*¡Qué ilusión* = how exciting!
Elegir = to choose	*Quitar* = to take off, remove
Enfadado = angry	*El regalo* = the gift, present
Enseñar = to show, teach	*Rico* = tasty, rich
La estancia = the stay	*Ser un éxito* = to be a success
Estar bueno = to be tasty	*La sierra* = the mountain
Estar harto = to be fed up	*El sillón* = the armchair
Estar a punto de = to be on the point of	*Tapear* = to have *tapas*
La habitación = the room, bedroom	*Tener prisa* = to be in a hurry
El intercambio = the exchange	*Tinto* = red (wine)
Lo que quieras = whatever you want	*Traer* = to bring
El panadero = the baker	*Verdaderamente* = really

Summary of unit

At the end of this unit

You should now be able to: understand more detailed spoken and written descriptions of people and make comparisons between people and things; describe yourself and other people, including personal characteristics, in both speech and writing; use a range of language, including quantifiers such as *poco*, *bastante* to modify their descriptions; respond appropriately in different social situations such as being a guest in a Spanish-speaking family or responding to the receipt of an invitation or gift.

You might also be able to: use a wider range of language in descriptions; write extended descriptions of people and places and say why you like or dislike them.

About the unit

In this unit you will learn to discuss your likes, dislikes and preferences as regards food and drink. You will also learn about quantities and be able to devise recipes.

New language content:

- direct object pronouns with things (*lo, la, los, las*)
- expressions of quantity
- using *tener hambre/sed*
- use of disjunctive pronoun with preposition, e.g. *para mí*

New contexts:

- food and drink
- likes, dislikes and preferences
- following and preparing recipes
- buying food
- restaurant/*tapas*
- Christmas food

Exercise 2.1 👂 ✍ 🗨

CD1: 12

¡Escucha!

Escucha esta conversación entre El Gordo y su amiga Elena. A ver si puedes hacer una lista de los diferentes tipos de comida que se mencionan. Toma apuntes abajo.

¿Alguien dice comida?

Apuntes:
La carne: . . . .
La paella: . . . .
Las verduras y las hortalizas: . . . .
La ensalada: . . . .
El postre: . . . .

Vocabulario
La carne = the meat
Las verduras = greens
Las hortalizas = vegetables
La ensalada = the salad
El postre = the dessert

Mañana, mañana

Spaniards have a reputation, sometimes unfairly, for putting things off. However, it is true to say that they do tend to take their meals much later than in this country. For example, whilst one could expect a restaurant in London to be fairly busy at one o'clock in the afternoon, in many areas of Spain a restaurant would not even be open at this time. The same applies to dinner and, to some extent, breakfast.

Now take a look at this conversation between Angela and Elena and answer the questions about meal-times afterwards.

Exercise 2.2

¡Lee!

Angela:	Bueno, Elena, ¿te apetece desayunar?
Elena:	¿Qué hora es?
Angela:	Son las ocho.
Elena:	Es un poco temprano, ¿no? En España no desayuno hasta las nueve.
Angela:	¿Y qué desayunas?
Elena:	Zumo de naranja, un café con leche y una tostada con aceite y tomate. ¡Qué rico!
Angela:	¡Qué asco! ¿Tostada con aceite? ¡Qué horror!
Elena:	¡Qué va! Está buenísimo. ¿Por qué no lo pruebas?
Angela:	No, gracias. ¿Y a qué hora almuerzas?
Elena:	Nunca comemos antes de las tres.
Angela:	¿Por qué?
Elena:	Porque mis padres no vuelven del trabajo hasta esa hora.
Angela:	¿Eso es normal?
Elena:	Sí. Muchas veces la gente deja de trabajar a eso de las dos y luego van a un bar a tomarse una cerveza antes de ir a casa para comer.
Angela:	¿Y qué sueles almorzar?
Elena:	Depende. De primer plato, sopa. Luego, normalmente, comemos carne con patatas fritas – pollo, solomillo, algo así. Y siempre tomamos ensalada. Y pan. El pan es muy importante.
Angela:	¿Y de postre?
Elena:	Bueno, yo prefiero flan, pero mi madre me dice que coma fruta porque está muy bien para la salud.
Angela:	¿Y qué te gusta beber?
Elena:	A mí, me gustaría cerveza, pero cuando como con mis padres tomo agua con gas; no les gusta que beba alcohol.

Contesta estas preguntas:

1. ¿Por qué Elena no quiere desayunar a las ocho?
2. ¿Qué piensa Angela de la tostada con aceite?
3. ¿Por qué Elena no almuerza antes de las tres?
4. ¿Qué hace mucha gente española antes de comer a mediodía?
5. ¿Qué tiene que comer Elena como postre, y por qué?
6. ¿Qué le gustaría beber a Elena, y por qué no puede hacerlo?

Vocabulario

Temprano = early
Desayunar = to have breakfast
El zumo = juice
La tostada = toast
¡Qué rico! = how delicious!
El aceite = oil
¡Qué asco! = how disgusting!
Probar (ue) = to try/sample
Almorzar = to have lunch
La salud = health

Exercise 2.3 ✍ 🗭

¡Habla!

Role-play. Working in pairs, construct a dialogue in Spanish in which you establish at what times you tend to eat breakfast, lunch and dinner. You should also provide information in terms of what your preferences are for these meals. Here is an example of the beginning of such a dialogue:

Ramón:	*¿A qué hora sueles desayunar, Jorge?*
Jorge:	*Suelo desayunar a las ocho y media, ¿y tú?*
Ramón:	*Yo, a las siete. ¿Qué prefieres desayunar?*
Jorge:	*Prefiero tostadas, muchas tostadas. ¿Y tú?*

You should write enough to cover all three areas, i.e. *el desayuno, el almuerzo, la cena*.

Exercise 2.4 ✍ 🗭

¡Escribe!

There are many food words that are similar in Spanish and English. You will know several already and will have come across some in exercise 2.1. See whether you can find the English equivalents of the Spanish words below. As you will see, some do not require an Einstein-like IQ:

1. *Atún, el*
2. *Coco, el*
3. *Coliflor, la*
4. *Ensalada, la*
5. *Espaguetis, los*
6. *Espinacas, las*
7. *Fruta, la*
8. *Hamburguesa, la*
9. *Jamón, el*
10. *Lasaña, la*
11. *Limón, el*
12. *Mandarina, la*
13. *Melón, el*
14. *Pasta, la*
15. *Patata, la*
16. *Pera, la*
17. *Piña, la*
18. *Pizza, la*
19. *Salmón, el*
20. *Sopa, la*
21. *Tomate, el*

Radical-changing verbs

You will often have come across this category of verb. You will also have noticed how some of these verbs, in particular *almorzar, preferir, querer* and *soler* are very useful when it comes to talking about food and drink. We shall now see whether you can remember how they work in the present tense.

Exercise 2.5 ✍️

¡Escribe!

Below, you are given a list of the subject pronouns and the 1st person singular of the verbs. Copy the table and write out the correct form of the verb in the remaining five persons.

	ALMORZAR	*PREFERIR*	*QUERER*	*SOLER*
Yo	*almuerzo*	*prefiero*	*quiero*	*suelo*
Tú	. . . .	. . . .	. . . .	. . . .
Él	. . . .	. . . .	. . . .	. . . .
Nosotros	. . . .	. . . .	. . . .	. . . .
Vosotros	. . . .	. . . .	. . . .	. . . .
Ellos	. . . .	. . . .	. . . .	. . . .

Exercise 2.6 ✍️ 💬

¡Escribe y habla!

Usando los verbos de arriba, inventa cuatro frases, cada una usando un verbo distinto.

*Ejemplo: Yo **suelo almorzar** a la una.*

Exercise 2.7 ✍️

¡Escribe!

Pon una palabra adecuada en cada hueco.

Pepe es un dormilón. Entonces no .... hasta las once. Le .... tomar una tostada y un .... con leche. También, normalmente, ... un zumo de naranja. No .... hasta las tres porque sus padres trabajan y no .... a casa hasta esa hora. Le .... beber vino, pero sus padres no le dejan. Por la noche .... a las diez.. Le gusta .... la carne y de .... helado de vainilla.

Vocabulario
Un dormilón = someone who likes
to sleep a lot

Exercise 2.8 🦻 ✍️ 🗨️

¡Escucha!

Una cena romántica

Escucha esta conversación entre Jorge, Elena y una camarera. Toma apuntes abajo.

Apuntes:

	Elena	**Jorge**
Primer plato:	. . . .	. . . .
Segundo plato:	. . . .	. . . .
Otros detalles:	. . . .	. . . .
	. . . .	. . . .
	. . . .	. . . .
	. . . .	. . . .

Vocabulario

Tomar nota = to take an order
¿Has decidido? = have you decided?
Cariño = darling
Apetecer = to feel like
El primer plato = the starter
El pescado = the fish
El segundo plato = the main course

De lujo = luxury, cordon bleu
¡Qué barbaridad! = how extraordinary!
La chuleta = the chop
Asado = roasted
El cerdo = the pig, pork
Poco hecho = rare
Medio hecho = medium

Exercise 2.9 📖 ✍️ 💬

¡Lee!

Lee este diálogo entre Jorge, Elena y la camarera y luego contesta las preguntas.

Más tarde en el restaurante...

Camarera:	¿Le ha gustado la ensalada, señorita?
Elena:	Mucho. Estaba buenísima.
Camarera:	¿Qué tal el solomillo, señor? ¿Estaba rico?
Jorge:	Sí, muy sabroso, pero los filetes eran un poco pequeños para mí.
Camarera:	Lo siento. ¿Les apetece algo de postre?
Elena:	Yo no puedo, gracias. Estoy llenísima.
Camarera:	¿De verdad? Tenemos tarta de queso, tarta de manzana, arroz con leche, mousse de chocolate.
Elena:	Es que no puedo.
Jorge:	Yo sí. ¿Tienen helado, o los restaurantes de lujo tampoco tienen helado?
Camarera:	Sí, señor, tenemos helado.
Jorge:	¿De qué sabores?
Camarera:	De fresa, vainilla, chocolate, de plátano con chocolate....
Jorge:	Póngame uno de fresa y vainilla, por favor. El chocolate me gusta, pero me da dolor de cabeza.
Camarera:	Muy bien. ¿Ya está?
Jorge:	No. Me apetece también arroz con leche. ¿Me lo trae después del helado, por favor?
Camarera:	¿Arroz con leche también?
Jorge:	Sí. ¿Hay algún problema?
Camarera:	Conmigo, no.
Jorge:	¿Quiere decir que yo sí tengo algún problema?
Camarera:	Claro que no señor.¿ Les pongo algo más de beber?
Jorge:	Sí, otra cerveza para mí. ¿Y tú, Elena?
Elena:	Yo quiero otra botella de agua con gas.
Camarera:	Ahora mismo.

Contesta las preguntas:

1. *¿Cuáles son las tres palabras en el texto para el inglés 'tasty'?*
2. *¿Por qué Elena no quiere postre?*
3. *¿Qué tipos de helado tienen en el restaurante?*
4. *¿Por qué a Jorge no le gusta el helado de chocolate?*
5. *¿Qué tipo de bebida piden?*

> **Vocabulario**
> *¿Le ha gustado...?* = did you like?
> *Estaba* = it was
> *La tarta de queso* = cheesecake
> *El arroz con leche* = rice pudding
> *El sabor* = taste
> *Ahora mismo* = right away

CD1: 16

Exercise 2.10

¡Escribe!
Traduce esta conversación entre Carlos y su hermano Manolo al español.

Carlos: I'm very hungry. I want to order.
Manolo: Me too. What do you feel like?
Carlos: I feel like a ham sandwich. And for you?
Manolo: For me, a hamburguer with lots of chips.
Carlos: What would you like to drink?
Manolo: I'll have a beer. And for you?
Carlos: I'd like a beer, but if Mum comes in....
Manolo: Better to order something else.
Carlos: Yes, I think you're right.

Exercise 2.11

¡Escribe y luego habla!
Role-play. Working in pairs, and using the format of the conversation above, invent a conversation between two Spanish friends who are hungry and thirsty and are talking about what they intend to eat and drink. Each person should have at least four lines.

Soler (ue)

As we discovered in Book 1, the radical-changing verb *soler (ue)* is particularly useful in terms of expressing the idea of doing something on a regular basis. So, for example, if I wanted to say 'I usually have breakfast at eight o'clock', rather than saying '*normalmente desayuno a las ocho*' (which is perfectly good and valid), I could translate this by saying '*suelo desayunar a las ocho*'. You can see how the verb is simply followed by an infinitive. Before going on to try out a few more sentences, we need to be clear that we remember how the verb works. Copy and fill in the correct parts of the verb alongside the following subject pronouns:

Yo	?	*Nosotros*	?
Tú	?	*Vosotros*	?
Él	?	*Ellos*	?

Now let's try a couple of exercises to reinforce its use.

Exercise 2.12 ✏️

¡Escribe!
Traduce estas frases al español.

1. I usually have lunch at one o'clock.
2. We usually order beer.
3. They are usually very hungry at four o'clock.
4. Do you (singular) usually eat dessert?
5. He usually has dinner with his brother.
6. Do you (singular) usually eat oranges?
7. Do you (singular) usually eat ham?
8. Do you (singular) usually eat sandwiches?

Now answer these last three questions (6-8), replacing the noun with the right pronoun. If you're not sure how to do this, look at this example:

¿Sueles comer plátanos? No suelo comerlos/no los suelo comer.

Exercise 2.13 ✏️

¡Escribe!
Using either the verb *soler* or the appropriate direct object pronoun, see if you can fill in the gaps in the text below. The first one has been done for you and is in bold.

*Carlos **suele** levantarse a las ocho. Baja con su hermano para tomar el desayuno. Los dos ……. comen juntos. A Manolo le gusta el café, pero siempre ……. toma con azúcar. Carlos prefiere leche. ……. toma muy, muy fría. Los hermanos van al mismo instituto y ……. almorzar juntos. Por la noche ……. tomar la cena con sus padres. ……. toman a eso de las nueve. Carlos ……. acostarse a las once, y su hermano ……. acostarse un poco más tarde.*

Exercise 2.14 ✏️

¡Escribe!

Now rewrite the passage in Exercise 2.13, replacing the verbs in the 3rd person singular and plural with the 1st person singular and plural. In other words, you should imagine that you are Carlos describing what you and your brother Manolo normally do. You must also remember that other words such as possessive adjectives (e.g. *su*) may need to change also. The passage would therefore begin:

> **Vocabulario**
> *Bajar* = to go downstairs
> *El azúcar* = sugar
> *Acostarse* = to go to bed

*Yo **suelo** levantar**me** a las ocho.*

Notice how the verb *levantarse* has changed to *levantarme*.

Vocabulario 2.1

Vocabulario 2.1

El aceite = the oil
Adecuado = adequate
Ahora mismo = right away
El ajo = the garlic
La albóndiga = the meatball
La almeja = the clam
Apetecer = to feel like
El arroz = the rice
El arroz con leche = rice-pudding
Asado = roast, roasted
El atún = tuna
La bebida = the drink
El calamar = the squid
El camarero/la camarera = the waiter, waitress
Cariño = darling
La carne = the meat
La cebolla = the onion
El cerdo = the pig, pork
La cerveza = the beer
El champiñón = the mushroom
La chuleta = the chop
El coco = the coconut
La coliflor = the cauliflower
El cordero = the lamb
De lujo = luxury, high-class
El dormilón = someone who sleeps a lot
El ejército = the army
La ensalada = the salad
Las espinacas = the spinach
El flan = the crème caramel
La fruta = the fruit
La gamba = the prawn
La gemela = the twin
La hamburguesa = the hamburguer
Las hortalizas = vegetables
El jamón = the ham
La judía verde = the green bean
La lasaña = the lasagne

La lechuga = the lettuce
El limón = the lemon
La mandarina = the mandarine
La manzana = the apple
Los mariscos = the shellfish
Medio hecho = medium (cooked)
El melón = the melon
La pasta = the pasta
La patata = the potato
La pechuga = the breast (chicken etc)
El pepino = the cucumber
La pera = the pear
El pimiento = the pepper
La piña = the pineapple
La pizza = the pizza
El plátano = the banana
Poco hecho = rare (cooked)
El pollo = the chicken
El postre = the dessert
El primer plato = the starter
Probar = to try, sample
¡Qué asco! = how disgusting!
¡Qué barbaridad! = how extraordinary!
Un refresco = a drink (non-alcoholic)
El sabor = the taste
El salmón = the salmon
El segundo plato = the main course
Soler = to be accustomed to
El solomillo = the sirloin
La sopa = the soup
Soportar = to tolerate
La tarta de queso = the cheesecake
La ternera = the veal
Tomar nota = to take an order
El tomate = the tomato
La tostada = toast
Las verduras = the greens
La zanahoria = the carrot
El zumo = the juice

Exercise 2.15

¡Escucha y escribe!

Lee las preguntas de abajo. Después, escucha la conversación entre Carmen y su amiga inglesa, Poppy, y contesta las preguntas.

1. ¿Qué tipo de comida hay en España, según Carmen?
2. ¿Por qué dice Carmen que no hay muchos restaurantes vegetarianos en España?
3. ¿Qué comida le gusta a Poppy?
4. ¿Qué tienen en común Jorge y Poppy?
5. ¿Qué tipo de comida se come en Inglaterra, según Poppy?
6. ¿Qué tipo de comida prefiere Carmen?
7. ¿Qué le gusta beber a Poppy?
8. ¿Qué son las 'copas'?

Exercise 2.16

¡Lee!

Lee esta conversación entre Jorge y su amigo Manolo.

Jorge:	Oye, Manolo, necesito tu ayuda. Como sabes, muy pronto va a ser el día de San Valentín, y Elena está muy enfadada conmigo.
Manolo:	¿Por qué?
Jorge:	Por lo del otro día en el restaurante.
Manolo:	Ah, sí. ¿Qué tal?
Jorge:	Fatal.
Manolo:	¿Por qué?
Jorge:	Por la camarera. ¡Qué mujer más antipática! Quiero arreglarlo. Quiero prepararle a Elena una comida buenísima. ¿Quieres ayudarme?
Manolo:	Claro. ¿Qué tipo de comida le gusta?
Jorge:	Le gusta todo: la comida italiana, la china, la francesa, incluso la comida inglesa.
Manolo:	¿La comida inglesa? ¿Está loca?
Jorge:	Un poco. El problema es que dice que está muy gorda y por eso siempre pide ensaladas.
Manolo:	¡Qué lástima!
Jorge:	¡De verdad!
Manolo:	Pero bueno, se puede hacer una ensalada muy rica.
Jorge:	¿Con qué?

Manolo:	Con los ingredientes normales. Para empezar: lechuga, tomate, cebolla, ajo, aceite de oliva. Luego se le pueden echar otras cosas. ¿Le gustan la fruta y la carne?
Jorge:	Sí, mucho.
Manolo:	Entonces, vamos a echarle piña, kiwi, plátano y pollo.
Jorge:	¿Piña, kiwi, plátano y pollo?
Manolo:	Sí, le va a encantar.
Jorge:	Espero que sí.

Vocabulario
El día de San Valentín = Saint Valentine's Day
Arreglar = to fix, put right
Ayudar = to help
Incluso = even
¡Qué lástima! = what a pity!
Echarle = to add to it

Ahora contesta estas preguntas:

1. *¿Por qué Jorge necesita la ayuda de Manolo?*
2. *¿Cómo describe a la camarera?*
3. *¿Por qué piensa Manolo que Elena está loca?*
4. *¿Por qué Elena siempre pide ensaladas?*
5. *¿Qué diferencia hay entre una ensalada normal y la ensalada de Manolo?*

Revision: ser and estar

You will have noticed that when describing food, if you want to say how good, or indeed bad, food is, you tend to use the verb *estar*. The reason for this is that food, sadly, does not **always** taste good – taste is a **changeable** characteristic. You will have studied this before, but let's see how much you remember.

Exercise 2.17 ✍️

¡Escribe!
*Usando **ser** o **estar**, traduce estas frases al español.*

1. This paella is fantastic.
2. She is from Spain.
3. The food is on the table.
4. These oranges are delicious.
5. Jorge is happy because the meat is good.

Una receta para Elena

The Spanish word *receta* means recipe. As well as being able to understand the ingredients, it is obviously fundamental to be able to understand how these different ingredients are to be used. On the next page you will find a vocabulary listing some of the most common words in this regard. They should also help you to do the two reading exercises, as well as help you to invent your own recipes.

Exercise 2.18

¡Lee y escribe!

Lee la receta de abajo y luego contesta las preguntas.

ENSALADA DE ARROZ Y PLÁTANO, de Karlos Arguiñano:

Ingredientes:

1 lechuga	Para el aliño:
100g. de arroz	Vinagre
2 plátanos	1 cucharadita de mostaza
50g. de pasas	Azúcar moreno
Agua	Sal
Un chorrito de zumo de limón	Orégano
Sal	Aceite de oliva

Elaboración:

Cuece el arroz en agua con un chorrito de zumo de limón y sal, pásalo por agua fría y escúrrelo bien.

Lava la lechuga y córtala en juliana, y a continuación colócala en una ensaladera junto con los plátanos pelados y cortados en rodajas. Agrega el arroz y mezcla bien todos los ingredientes. Añade las pasas.

En un recipiente aparte, bate una cucharadita de mostaza con un poco de vinagre, sal y una pizca de azúcar. Agrega el aceite y el orégano, mezcla bien y aliña con esto la ensalada.

Contesta esta preguntas:

1. ¿Cómo se prepara el arroz?
2. ¿Qué se hace con la lechuga?
3. ¿Qué se hace después de colocar la lechuga y los plátanos en la ensaladera?
4. ¿Para qué se usa el recipiente aparte?

Vocabulario

Una pasa = a prune
El vinagre = the vinegar
La mostaza = the mustard
El azúcar moreno = brown sugar
El orégano = orégano
La elaboración = the preparation
Una ensaladera = a salad bowl
Una rodaja = a slice
Un recipiente = a container
Aparte = separate
Pelado = peeled/skinned

Vocabulario

Cocer (ue) = to cook	Aliñar = to dress, season
Lavar = to wash	Escurrir = to drain, strain
Cortar = to cut	Incorporar = to add
Colocar = to put, place	Dejar cocer a fuego suave = to let simmer
Agregar = to add	Batir = to beat, mix, whisk
Añadir = to add	Una pizca = a pinch (of salt), a trace
Mezclar = to mix	Una cucharadita = a teaspoonful
Pelar = to peel	Un chorrito = a few drops of
Remover = to stir	Cortar en juliana = to cut into thin shreds
Hervir = to boil	Pasar por agua fría = to run under cold water
Escalfar = to poach	El aliño = the dressing
Rehogar = to sauté	Un gramo (g) = a gramme

Exercise 2.19

CD1: 19

¡Escucha, toma apuntes y luego habla!

Escucha esta conversación entre Carmen y su amiga Lucía sobre cómo hacer una paella. Toma apuntes abajo.

Apuntes:

Ingredientes: . . . .

. . . .

. . . .

Elaboración: . . . .

. . . .

. . . .

Una paella

Exercise 2.20

CD1: 20

¡Escribe y luego habla!

Role-play. Working in pairs, and using some of the words you have learnt for both ingredients and preparation, invent a recipe of your own. One person should be responsible for reading out the ingredients, whilst the other will be responsible for giving instructions as to how the dish should be prepared.

Exercise 2.21

CD1: 21

¡Escucha, toma apuntes y luego habla!

1. Listen to the conversation in the restaurant and take notes on what Antonio and María order.

Apuntes:

	Antonio:	**María:**
Primer plato:	. . . .	. . . .
Segundo plato:	. . . .	. . . .
Bebida:	. . . .	. . . .

2. Role-play. Working in pairs, now see whether you can invent a more detailed dialogue between two people ordering a meal in a restaurant. As with the scene between Antonio and María, see whether you are able to progress from ordering a single item to a full meal, e.g. *de primero….de segundo….de postre.*

Exercise 2.22 📖

¡Lee!

The lines below are all part of a brief conversation between a waiter and a client in a cafeteria. They are, however, all jumbled up. See whether you can rewrite the dialogue in its correct sequence.

Camarero:	*¿Quiere una ensalada o alguna guarnición con la carne?*
Cliente:	*Media botella de vino tinto y un botellín de agua con gas.*
Camarero:	*Muy bien señor.*
Cliente:	*Unas patatas fritas.*
Camarero:	*Buenos días. ¿Qué va a tomar?*
Cliente:	*Poco hecho por favor.*
Camarero:	*¿Y de beber?*
Cliente:	*De primero, la sopa de pescado y de segundo, un filete de ternera.*
Camarero:	*¿Cómo lo quiere?*

> **Vocabulario**
> *La guarnición:* usually a garnish or a selection of vegetables to go with a meat or fish dish
> *Un botellín* = a small bottle

La merienda

Throughout this unit, we have looked at the subject of food and drink in terms of the major meals in the day, i.e. *el desayuno, el almuerzo, la cena*. We have also mentioned the Spanish habit of eating *tapas*, primarily as a prelude to a meal, in particular, lunch. However, we must not forget one further custom: *la merienda*. This daily habit usually occurs in the late afternoon or early evening, some time before the evening meal. *La merienda* is best described as a snack which, if taken outside home, usually takes the form of a coffee or hot chocolate and, for example, *churros* (long fritters made out of flour and water). If having *la merienda* at home, one might choose to have some biscuits or a sandwich and perhaps a *café con leche*. There is a specific verb associated with this custom: *merendar*.

Exercise 2.23

¡Escribe!
Usando las palabras de abajo, pon la palabra correcta en cada hueco.

zumo	mucha	beber	ingredientes	siento	tal	quieres
una	apetece	tomar	qué	vale	quiero	tú

Pepe: ¿....... merendar?

Yolanda: No, tengo .... hambre. Voy a pedir algunas tapas.

Pepe: ¿....... tapas quieres?

Yolanda: Voy a .... pollo al ajillo y ensaladilla rusa.

Pepe: ¿Qué ......tiene la ensaladilla rusa?

Yolanda: Creo que mayonesa, atún, gambas, patatas y aceitunas.

Pepe: A mí también me .... También .... boquerones en vinagre y huevos rellenos.

Yolanda: ¿Qué .... unos mejillones al vapor?

Pepe: .... ¿Qué quieres ....?

Yolanda: Yo, un .... de naranja. ¿Y ....?

Pepe: Yo, ... cerveza.

Yolanda: Lo .... No puedes.

> **Vocabulario**
> *Pollo al ajillo* = chicken flavoured with garlic
> *La mayonesa* = the mayonnaise
> *La aceituna* = the olive
> *El boquerón* = the anchovy
> *Huevos rellenos* = eggs with a stuffing, usually tuna, tomato and mayonnaise
> *Mejillones al vapor* = steamed mussels

La Navidad

Spaniards celebrate Christmas in a slightly different way from us. In terms of the giving and receiving of presents, traditionally the important time has always been the night of January 5th and the morning of January 6th. These dates coincide, of course, with the arrival of the three wise men in Bethlehem. As far as meals are concerned, there is again a difference. The important family meal is celebrated as dinner on Christmas Eve. Whilst it is common for turkey (*pavo*) to be eaten as the main course, the first course would traditionally take the form of *mariscos* (seafood), for example *langostinos* (large prawns) or *gambas* (prawns). Dessert might involve some type of fruit such as *piña*, and the meal would definitely end with *mantecados* ('lardy cakes'). One would probably also tuck into *turrón* (nougat). As far as drink is concerned, it would be typical to have some *cava* which is a sparkling wine, not unlike champagne. Wine is a must with the meal, and it would be normal practice to knock back a few drops of *anís* (anisette) afterwards. In short, you could definitely expect to have put on a few pounds, if not stones, after the Christmas festivities.

CD1: 23

Exercise 2.24 👂 ✍ 💬

¡Escucha!

Escucha este diálogo entre Elvira y una dependienta en Hipercor y toma apuntes abajo sobre la comida y bebida que Elvira necesita para la cena de Nochebuena.

Apuntes:
Comida: . . . .
Bebida: . . . .
¿Dónde?: . . . .

Vocabulario
Una dependienta = a shop assistant
La Nochebuena = Christmas Eve

Vocabulario 2.2

Vocabulario 2.2

La aceituna = the olive	*Incluso* = even
Agregar = to add	*Incorporar* = to add
Aliñar = to dress (salads etc)	*Indio* = Indian
El aliño = the dressing	*El ingrediente* = the ingredient
Aparte = separate	*Italiano* = Italian
Arreglar = to fix, put right	*El kiwi* = the kiwi
El azúcar = the sugar	*Lavar* = to wash
El azúcar moreno = brown sugar	*La mayonesa* = the mayonnaise
Batir = to beat, mix, whisk	*Mejicano* = Mexican
El boquerón = the anchovy	*El mejillón* = the mussel
El botellín = the little bottle	*Mezclar* = to mix
Chino = Chinese	*La mostaza* = the mustard
Un chorrito = a few drops of	*Remover* = to stir
Colocar = to put, place	*La Nochebuena* = Christmas Eve
La copa = the glass, spirit with mixer	*El orégano* = the oregano
Cortar en juliana = to cut into thin strips	*La pasa* = the prune
Una cucharadita = a teaspoonful	*Pasar por agua* = to run under water
Una dependienta = a shop assistant	*Pelar* = to peel
Echar = to add	*Una pizca* = a pinch (of salt)
La elaboración = the preparation	*¡Qué lástima!* = what a shame/pity!
Escalfar = to poach	*La receta* = the recipe
Enfadado = angry	*El recipiente* = the container
La ensaladera = the salad bowl	*Rehogar* = to sauté
Escurrir = to drain	*La rodaja* = the slice
Francés = French	*El ron* = the rum
Un gramo = a gram	*La sal* = the salt
La guarnición = the garnish	*La tónica* = the tonic
Hervir = to boil	*El vapor* = the steam
El huevo = the egg	*El vinagre* = the vinegar
El huevo relleno = the egg with a stuffing	

Summary of unit

At the end of this unit

You should now be able to: understand spoken and written descriptions of food and recipes; state your preferences for food and drink, including cuisines from different countries; order a meal or *tapas* for yourself or others from memory, or tell someone what you would like.

You might also be able to: understand more complex spoken and written descriptions of food and recipes; state more detailed preferences for food and drink.

About the unit

In this unit you will learn to talk and write about feeling well and unwell and to give and receive simple advice about medical matters. You will be able to read and write about maintaining a healthy routine and lifestyle.

New language content:

- parts of the body
- structure with *doler*
- further expressions with *tener*
- structures such as *tener que* + infinitive, *hay que* + infinitive

New contexts:

- ailments, illnesses and remedies
- visiting the doctor, chemist or dentist
- healthy lifestyle

El cuerpo

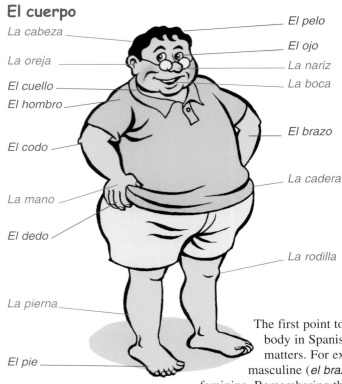

La cabeza
La oreja
El cuello
El hombro
El codo
La mano
El dedo
La pierna
El pie

El pelo
El ojo
La nariz
La boca
El brazo
La cadera
La rodilla

> **Vocabulario**
> *La cabeza* = the head
> *El pelo* = the hair
> *El ojo* = the eye
> *La nariz* = the nose
> *La boca* = the mouth
> *El cuello* = the neck
> *El hombro* = the shoulder
> *La oreja* = the ear
> *El brazo* = the arm
> *La mano* = the hand
> *El dedo* = the finger
> *El codo* = the elbow
> *La cadera* = the hip
> *La pierna* = the leg
> *La rodilla* = the knee
> *El pie* = the foot

The first point to make about the different parts of the body in Spanish is that, unlike in English, **gender** matters. For example, while the word for arm is masculine (*el brazo*), the word for leg (*la pierna*) is feminine. Remembering the correct gender is additionally important as, unlike in English, one tends to use the definite article in Spanish rather than the possessive adjective. For example, if you wanted to say 'my hand hurts' in Spanish, you would not use the possessive adjective *mi*. You would say '*me duele **la** mano*'.

CD1:
24

Exercise 3.1 📖 ✍️ 💬

¡Lee!

Lee este diálogo entre Jorge y el médico y luego contesta las preguntas.

Médico:	Buenos días Jorge.
Jorge:	Buenos días.
Médico:	Hace mucho tiempo que no te veo. ¿Qué tal?
Jorge:	Regular. Últimamente me duele mucho el estómago.
Médico:	¿Desde cuándo?
Jorge:	Hoy es miércoles..... Desde el domingo por la mañana.
Médico:	¿Te duele algo más?
Jorge:	Bueno, la espalda de vez en cuando.
Médico:	Estás un poco más gordo, ¿no? ¿Qué comes?

Jorge:	Como más o menos lo mismo, pero estoy comiendo más hamburguesas y más patatas fritas.
Médico:	¿Y galletas, mantecados, turrón?
Jorge:	Sí, como estamos en Navidad, estoy comiendo muchas de esas cosas, también.
Médico:	¿Y fruta?
Jorge:	No me gusta nada.
Médico:	Tienes que comer fruta, hombre. Es muy buena para la salud. Vamos a tener que cambiar tu dieta.
Jorge:	No doctor, por favor. Cualquier cosa menos eso.
Médico:	Lo siento, Jorge.

Contesta estas preguntas:

1. ¿Qué parte del cuerpo le duele a Jorge?
2. ¿Desde cuándo tiene este dolor?
3. ¿Qué dice el médico sobre el aspecto físico de Jorge?
4. La dieta de Jorge es un poco diferente ahora. ¿Cómo?
5. ¿Por qué está comiendo tantas galletas, mantecados y turrón?
6. ¿Por qué tiene que comer fruta?

> **Vocabulario**
> *Últimamente* = recently
> *La espalda* = the back
> *De vez en cuando* = from time to time
> *Lo mismo* = the same thing
> *La salud* = health
> *La dieta* = the diet (one's usual food intake)
> *El mantecado* = ice cream, lardy cake
> *Cualquier cosa* = anything
> *Menos* = except

The verb doler

Doler is a crucial verb when it comes to describing ailments and pain. As you will have noticed, it is yet another radical-changing verb. You may also have spotted that it works in the same way as verbs like *gustar*. It is therefore important to remember that the verb will be preceded by the indirect object pronouns *me, te, le, nos, os, les* and is only ever likely to be used in the third person, i.e. *duele* and *duelen*.

Exercise 3.2

¡Escribe!
Traduce las frases de abajo al español.

Ejemplos:
My hands hurt = *me duelen las manos.*
His head hurts = *le duele la cabeza.*

1. My feet hurt.
2. Does your head hurt?
3. Their legs hurt.
4. Our hands hurt.
5. His knee hurts.

Exercise 3.3

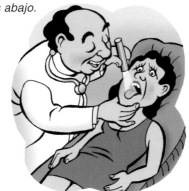

¡Escucha, toma apuntes y luego habla!
Escucha este diálogo entre Carmen y su médico, y toma apuntes abajo.

Apuntes:

Dolores: . . . .

Diagnóstico: . . . .

Medicamento y consejo: . . . .

Vocabulario

Encontrarse bien/mal = to feel well/unwell
El síntoma = the symptom
Sentirse = to feel
A lo mejor = perhaps
El virus = the virus
Inflamado = inflamed
El termómetro = the thermometer
Los antibióticos = the antibiotics
Hay que = one must
La pastilla = the pill
Tener fiebre = to have a temperature
El dolor = the ache, pain
El diagnóstico = the diagnosis
El consejo = the advice

The imperative: revision

The imperative is another term for a command. You may have noticed on listening to the dialogue between Carmen and her doctor that the imperative was used by the doctor when he asked her to lie down (*échate*) and also when he asked her to open her mouth (*abre la boca*). You will see that the verb in each case uses the same form as the third person of the present tense. This is generally the rule to adopt when you want to use the singular imperative in the familiar (or informal) form. There are other types of command and we will look at those later.

Exercise 3.4

¡Escribe!
By applying the guidelines above on how to form the familiar imperative, give the singular commands for the following verbs:

1.   *hablar*
2.   *comer*
3.   *beber*
4.   *dormir*

Exercise 3.5

¡Escribe y luego habla!
Role-play. Working in pairs, and using the dialogue between Carmen and her doctor as a model, invent an exchange between a patient and his/her doctor. The conversation should contain questions from the doctor, trying to ascertain the problem(s), and suitable responses from the patient in terms of how long they have been suffering and what the nature of their ailment is. Try to incorporate one or two uses of the imperative as well as advice from the doctor as regards how the problem should be dealt with.

Exercise 3.6

¡Lee!

Lee este diálogo entre Elena y su dentista y luego contesta las preguntas.

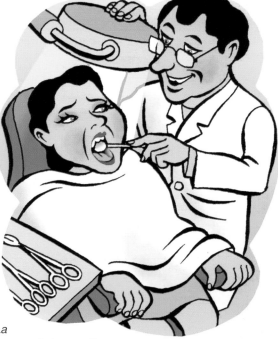

Dentista: Hola Elena. Tanto tiempo sin verte. ¿Te pasa algo?

Elena: Sí, me duele mucho este diente, aquí, a la derecha.

Dentista: Abre la boca bien, por favor……….Ah sí, esta muela de aquí. ¿Con qué frecuencia te lavas los dientes?

Elena: Siempre me los lavo por la mañana después de desayunar, y, por la noche, antes de acostarme.

Dentista: ¿Usas hilo dental?

Elena: No.

Dentista: Pues, hay que hacerlo. El hilo dental está muy bien para evitar la formación de caries. Úsalo por la mañana y por la noche, y compra un enjuague también. La higiene bucal es muy importante. ¿Tienes una dieta sana?

Elena: Bastante, pero me gustan mucho las galletas y las chucherías.

Dentista: Tienes que comer menos cosas dulces. El azúcar perjudica mucho la dentadura.

Elena: Vale. ¿Y qué hacemos con este diente, entonces?

Dentista: Hay que empastarlo.

Elena: Eso me va a doler mucho, ¿no?

Dentista: No. Te pongo anestesia local. No te va a doler nada. Pero tienes que tener más cuidado con los dientes. Y hay que venir más de una vez cada tres años.

Contesta estas preguntas:

1. ¿Por qué Elena necesita ver al dentista?
2. ¿Cuántas veces al día se lava los dientes?
3. ¿Por qué hay que usar el hilo dental?
4. ¿Qué más consejos le da el dentista a Elena?
5. ¿Qué va a hacer el dentista con el diente enfermo?
6. ¿Por qué no le va a doler?
7. ¿Cuál es el último consejo del dentista?

Vocabulario

El diente = the tooth	*El enjuague* = mouthwash
La muela = the molar tooth	*La higiene bucal* = dental hygiene
La frecuencia = the frequency	*Sano* = healthy
Acostarse = to go to bed	*Dulce* = sweet
El hilo dental = the dental floss	*Perjudicar* = to damage
Evitar = to avoid, prevent	*Empastar* = to fill a tooth
La caries = the plaque	*Tener cuidado* = to take care

Vocabulario 3.1

Vocabulario 3.1

Los antibióticos = the antibiotics
La boca = the mouth
El brazo = the arm
La cabeza = the head
La cadera = the hip
La caries = plaque
El codo = the elbow
El consejo = the advice
Cualquier cosa = anything
El cuello = the neck
De vez en cuando = from time to time
El diagnóstico = the diagnosis
La dieta = the diet
El diente = the tooth
Doler = to hurt
El dolor = the pain, ache
Dulce = sweet
Empastar = to fill
Encontrarse bien/mal = to feel good/bad
El enjuague = the mouthwash
La espalda = the back
Evitar = to avoid

La frecuencia = the frequency
La galleta = biscuit
Hay que = one has to
La higiene bucal = the oral hygiene
El hilo dental = the dental floss
El hombro = the shoulder
Inflamado = inflamed
Lo mismo = the same thing
La mano = the hand
El medicamento = the medication
La muela = the molar tooth
La pastilla = the pill
Perjudicar = to harm, damage
El pie = the foot
La pierna = the leg
La rodilla = the knee
La salud = the health
Sentirse = to feel
El síntoma = the symptom
Tener cuidado = to take care
El termómetro = the thermometer
Últimamente = recently

Exercise 3.7

¡Lee!
Read this letter from Ana to an agony aunt in a newspaper.

Querida Susana:

Te escribo para pedirte ayuda sobre un problema que tengo desde hace bastante tiempo. El problema es que estoy cada vez más gorda y no sé qué hacer. Intento hacer un poco de ejercicio y no comer demasiada comida grasa, por ejemplo: los dulces y las patatas fritas. También, muchas veces me pongo a régimen. Voy a la piscina de vez en cuando y hago footing una vez al mes. Como bastante fruta y ensalada, pero me gustan mucho el pan y las galletas, y, sobre todo, el chocolate. No suelo desayunar mucho y tampoco como demasiado a mediodía; entonces, a menudo me inflo de comer por la noche. Intento no tomar mucho alcohol, pero me encanta la cerveza. También me gusta la coca-cola. A ver si puedes decirme lo que tengo que hacer para adelgazar y no engordar tanto.

Un abrazo.
Ana

Contesta estas preguntas:

1.   *¿Por qué Ana le escribe a Susana?*
2.   *¿Qué hace para intentar no estar gorda?*
3.   *¿Por qué suele comer mucho por la noche?*
4.   *¿Qué bebidas le gustan?*

> **Vocabulario**
> *Cada vez más* = more and more
> *Intentar* = to try to
> *Hacer ejercicio* = to do exercise
> *La comida grasa* = fatty foods
> *Ponerse a régimen* = to go on a diet
> *Hacer footing* = to go jogging
> *Inflarse de comer* = to stuff oneself
> *Adelgazar* = to lose weight
> *Engordar* = to put on weight

Exercise 3.8

¡Escribe!

Now imagine that you are the agony aunt, and write a reply to Ana in which you should offer advice as to how she might overcome her problem.

The imperative – part 2

We have previously established that, in order to form the singular familiar imperative or command, one usually uses the third person singular of the present tense of the verb in question. So, when the dentist asked Elena to open her mouth he said '*Abre la boca*'. However, if Elena had been a new patient, and he was therefore meeting her for the first time, he would have used the polite imperative which is very slightly different. In this case, he would have said '*Abra*' rather than '*Abre*'. Again, infuriatingly, there are verbs that have strange, irregular polite commands, but, generally speaking, there is a rule, as we met in Book 1, which one can follow. Now, in the exercise that follows, make a list of all the polite commands and then establish what the pattern is.

CD1:
27

Exercise 3.9

¡Lee!

Read this dialogue between María and a pharmacist and then give a list of all the examples you can find of the polite form of the imperative.

Farmacéutico:	*Buenos días señora. ¿En qué puedo ayudarle?*
María:	*Tengo un dolor de cabeza tremendo. Me encuentro fatal.*
Farmacéutico:	*Siéntese, por favor. Tome, aquí tiene usted una silla.*
María:	*Muchas gracias.*
Farmacéutico:	*De nada. ¿Le duele algo más?*
María:	*No, solamente la cabeza, pero me duele muchísimo. Demasiado vino anoche.*
Farmacéutico:	*Bueno, espere unos segundos. Le voy a dar unas pastillas…..Tome una, dos veces al día, con la comida. Descanse mucho, beba mucha agua, y coma algo ligero.*

> **Vocabulario**
> *Tremendo* = awful, frightful
> *Demasiado* = too much
> *Descansar* = to rest
> *Ligero* = light

CD1:
28

Exercise 3.10 ✍

¡Escribe!

Rewrite the conversation between María and the pharmacist on the assumption that they know each other. You will therefore need not only to think about the commands, but also about other uses of verbs. You will also need to think about pronouns, and indeed the mode of address. For example, the first line would now read:

Farmacéutico: *Buenos días María. ¿En qué puedo ayudarte?*

A recording of the amended conversation is available on the CD.

Exercise 3.11 📖 ✍ 🗨

¡Lee!
Lee esta carta de Susana a Ana y luego contesta las preguntas.

> *Querida Ana:*
>
> *Muchas gracias por tu carta. Primero, tengo que decirte que no debes preocuparte demasiado. Por supuesto, hay que cuidar la imagen bastante, y la salud es muy importante, pero también es importante no obsesionarse con el físico. Dicho esto, vamos a ver si te puedo ayudar. Como tú reconoces en tu carta, hay que hacer ejercicio, y yo creo que tienes que intentar ir a la piscina más a menudo. Además, en lugar de hacer footing una vez al mes, hace falta intentar practicarlo más a menudo. Hay que hacer un esfuerzo mental, no solamente un esfuerzo físico. También hay otras maneras de ponerse en forma. El ciclismo, por ejemplo, está muy bien, y no perjudica al cuerpo.*
>
> *En cuanto a la comida, está muy bien comer fruta y ensalada, pero tienes que comer menos pan, galletas y chocolate. Engordan mucho. También debes cambiar tus costumbres. El desayuno es la comida más importante, por lo tanto tienes que hacer un esfuerzo y comer más por la mañana. También hace falta comer bien a mediodía. El cuerpo necesita energía y la comida es super importante para eso. Además, si comes más durante el día, no vas a tener que inflarte por la noche, lo cual es muy malo para la salud.*
>
> *En fin, no debe ser una obsesión, pero hay varias cosas que tienes que tratar de cambiar.*
>
> *Un abrazo fuerte.*
>
> *Susana*

Contesta estas preguntas:

1. *¿Cuál es el primer consejo que Susana le da a Ana?*
2. *¿Qué dice Susana sobre el ejercicio que hace Ana?*
3. *¿Por qué dice que el ciclismo es una buena manera de hacer ejercicio?*
4. *¿Qué dice Susana sobre la dieta de Ana?*
5. *¿Por qué dice que es muy importante comer más durante el día?*
6. *¿Qué tipo de persona parece ser Susana y por qué?*

Vocabulario

Preocuparse = to worry
Por supuesto = naturally, of course
La imagen = the image,
   physical appearance
Obsesionarse = to become obsessed
Dicho esto = having said that
Reconocer = to realise, admit
A menudo = often

Además = besides
En lugar de = instead of
Hacer falta = to be necessary
Un esfuerzo = an effort
Ponerse en forma = to get fit
En cuanto a = as regards
Por lo tanto = therefore
Super importante = vital

Hay que, tener que, deber, hacer falta

As you may have noticed on reading Susana's letter to Ana, the above verbs can all be used to give both positive and negative advice. For example, at the beginning of her letter, Susana writes '*hay que cuidar la imagen*' and towards the end she says '*no debe ser una obsesión*'. As you can see, in each case the verb is followed by an infinitive. This is also the case with *tener que* and *hacer falta*. One difference to point out is that both *hay que* and *hacer falta* are impersonal. So, strictly speaking, when Susana says '*hay que cuidar la imagen*', she is really saying 'one has to look after one's appearance'. She is not referring specifically to Ana; it is more of a general observation. Both *tener que* and *deber* can be used impersonally if one puts the word *se* before them. In this way, Susana *could* have said, for example, '*se tiene que cuidar la imagen*'.

Let's see whether you can now use these verbs both positively and negatively in terms of offering advice on healthy living. Using your own brains, in the exercise below, complete sentences 1-4 to offer positive advice, and sentences 5-8 to say what people should not do. Look at these examples to help you:

Hay que comer bastante por la mañana = one should eat sufficiently in the morning.

No se deben comer demasiadas galletas = one should not eat too many biscuits.

Exercise 3.12 ✐ 🗨

¡Escribe!
Complete the sentences below, offering advice on how to achieve a healthy lifestyle.
Ejemplo: Hay que beber mucha agua.

1. *Hay que ......*
2. *Se tiene que ......*
3. *Hace falta ......*
4. *Se debe ......*
5. *No hay que ......*
6. *No se tiene que ......*
7. *No hace falta ......*
8. *No se debe ......*

Horóscopo

Aries:

Salud: Tienes que hacer más ejercicio y no ser tan perezoso.
Trabajo: Vas a tener una semana muy difícil.

Libra:

Salud: Te va a doler todo el cuerpo y vas a tener mucha fiebre.
Trabajo: Vas a perder tu trabajo.

Tauros:

Salud: Estupenda.
Trabajo: Maravilloso.

Escorpio:

Salud: Fabulosa.
Trabajo: Tienes que ser más tolerante.

Géminis:

Salud: Bastante buena.
Trabajo: No seas tan pesimista.

Sagitario:

Salud: Buena.
Trabajo: Regular.

Cáncer:

Salud: Buena.
Trabajo: Horizonte bueno.

Capricornio:

Salud: Excelente.
Trabajo: Vas a tener una semana un poco difícil.

Leo:

Salud: Vas a tener una semana fabulosa.
Trabajo: Tienes que pensar más en el futuro.

Acuario:

Salud: Buena.
Trabajo: Una semana muy productiva.

Virgo:

Salud: Ni buena ni mala.
Trabajo: Tienes que ser más ambicioso.

Piscis:

Salud: Bastante buena.
Trabajo: Muy bueno.

Exercise 3.13

¡Lee!

Lee bien el horóscopo de arriba y, sin usar el diccionario, trata de contestar estas preguntas.

1. ¿Qué signo no va a tener buena salud?
2. ¿Qué signo tiene que intentar hacer algo más?
3. ¿Qué signos tienen una salud estupenda?
4. ¿Quién va a tener la peor semana con respecto al trabajo?

Vocabulario
Mantenerse en forma = to keep fit
Procurar = to try
El punto débil = the weak point/spot
Equilibrado = balanced
Disfrutar = to enjoy
Montar a caballo = to go riding
Relajarse = to relax

Exercise 3.14

¡Escucha!

Escucha a Carlos, a María y a Carla, y toma apuntes sobre lo que dicen.

Apuntes:

	Carlos	**María**	**Carla**
Comida:	. . . .	. . . .	. . . .
Punto débil:	. . . .	. . . .	. . . .
Bebida:	. . . .	. . . .	. . . .
Deportes:	. . . .	. . . .	. . . .
¿Cuántas veces?:	. . . .	. . . .	. . . .
El futuro:	. . . .	. . . .	. . . .
Otros:	. . . .	. . . .	. . . .

Contesta estas preguntas:

1.   ¿Qué le gusta comer?
2.   ¿Cuál es su punto débil?
3.   ¿Qué le gusta beber?
4.   ¿Qué deportes le gustan?
5.   ¿Cuántas veces los practica?
6.   ¿Qué quiere hacer en el futuro?
7.   ¿Qué otras cosas le parecen importantes?

Exercise 3.15

CD1: 29-31

¡Lee!

¡Lee el artículo de abajo y contesta las preguntas.

TOXICOMANÍAS: PLAN NACIONAL SOBRE DROGAS

El 78% de los adolescentes españoles consume alcohol y el 20% fuma cada día, según un sondeo.

Alcohol y tabaco son drogas habituales para los estudiantes españoles de entre 14 y 18 años. Según la primera encuesta a escolares del Plan Nacional sobre Drogas (PNSD), el 78,5% reconoce beber, y de ellos un 95,4% lo hace el fin de semana. El 20% fuma cotidianamente, con una media de nueve cigarrillos al día. En otras drogas, la principal es el hachís (12% al mes). Las sustancias más temidas para ellos son la heroína y la cocaína, aunque asocian el riesgo, más a la frecuencia del consumo que al tipo de droga.

Dos drogas legales, alcohol y tabaco, son las más consumidas por los adolescentes españoles, según una encuesta del PNSD realizada a finales de 1994 entre 21.094 escolares de 395 centros públicos y privados de enseñanza secundaria, bachillerato y formación profesional (FP).

Los chicos beben más: un 14,2%, más de dos días a la semana, mientras que las chicas son un 6,2%. El consumo se produce mayoritariamente el fin de semana (un 95,4%). Toman sobre todo cerveza, y sólo, esporádicamente, vino. Un 38,6% de los estudiantes de 14 y 15 años bebe en discotecas, y un 56%, en bares, lo cual demuestra que los bares se saltan impunemente la prohibición de vender alcohol a menores.

"No es algo que esté teóricamente prohibido", dijo Carlos López Riaño, delegado del Gobierno para el PNSD, al presentar la encuesta con Álvaro Marchesi, secretario de Estado de Educación. "Es que está claramente prohibido. Los hosteleros tienen que sentarse a pensar soluciones con la Administración y con las organizaciones ciudadanas. No puede ser que haya diversos grados de rigor en los municipios. Y la familia es cada vez más importante".

Al anunciar el carácter anual que a partir de ahora tendrá la encuesta, Marchesi y Carlos López Riaño consideraron que, "por fortuna, nuestro sistema educativo está al margen de las drogas", aunque López Riaño añadió que "otra cosa es lo que pase a la puerta del centro escolar". Con la edad aumenta el consumo de cualquier droga. En cuanto al alcohol, por ejemplo, la proporción de bebedores semanales aumenta de un 17,3% a los 14 años, hasta un 54,4% a los 18. Un 43,5% de los encuestados se ha emborrachado alguna vez, y un 24% lo ha hecho el último mes.

El tabaco también es habitual entre ellos. La mayor parte de los escolares fumadores diarios consume de 6 a 10 cigarrillos, o sea, una media de 9,2. También la edad resulta clave: a los 14 años los fumadores diarios son un 8,1%, pero a los 18 llegan al 36,2%: pasan de 7 a 11,4 cigarrillos al día. Las chicas fumadoras son más: diariamente, el 24,1% y un 17,1% de chicos. Un 32,9% de chicas dice haber fumado durante el último mes, frente a un 23,4% de chicos. Sin embargo, de quienes consumen más de medio paquete al día, un 35,4% son chicos y un 20,3% chicas. La edad media de inicio al consumo es de 13 a 14 años.

La droga más extendida, aparte del alcohol y del tabaco, es el hachís (Cannabis): un 12,2% de los escolares dice haberlo consumido alguna vez en el último mes.

Miguel Bayón
El País, 26 de junio, 1995

Below, you will find a number of percentages and a number of statements in Spanish. See whether you can match up the percentages with the correct statement. There may be words you do not understand. Just do your best to understand the gist of the Spanish (not something we often let you get away with!).

1.	78.5%	A.	*Tienen 18 años y beben alcohol cada semana.*
2.	95.4%	B.	*Son los estudiantes que fuman el hachís cada mes.*
3.	20%	C.	*Son las chicas que tienen 18 años y que fuman diariamente (cada día).*
4.	12%	D.	*Son los estudiantes que reconocen beber alcohol.*
5.	14.2%	E.	*Son los chicos que beben más de dos días cada semana.*
6.	38.6%	F.	*Son los chicos que reconocen beber alcohol los fines de semana.*
7.	54.4%	G.	*Son los jóvenes de 14 años que fuman cada día.*
8.	8.1%	H.	*Son los estudiantes entre 14 y 18 años que fuman cada día.*
9.	24.1%	I.	*Son los chicos que fuman más de medio paquete al día.*
10.	35.4%	J.	*Son los estudiantes de 14 y 15 años que beben en discotecas.*

Exercise 3.16

¡Lee!

Lee esta carta de Ana a Susana y luego contesta las preguntas:

> *Querida Susana:*
>
> *Muchas gracias por tu carta y por tu consejo. Estoy haciendo mucho más ejercicio ahora y también estoy comiendo mucho mejor. Primero, hago footing todos los días antes de ir al colegio, y después de comer un desayuno más grande. Voy a la piscina tres veces por semana. Además, tengo una bici nueva y doy una vuelta tres o cuatro veces por semana. Peso seis kilos menos.*
>
> *Ya no como ni galletas ni chocolate. Como pan, pero solamente con las comidas. Como bastante por la mañana y a mediodía y mucho menos por la noche. Creo que estoy más guapa porque Juan, el chico más guapo de la clase, se fija mucho en mí ahora – antes, no. Estoy contentísima.*
>
> *Un abrazo.*
>
> *Ana*

Vocabulario
Pesar = to weigh
Fijarse en = to take notice of
Funcionar = to work

Contesta estas preguntas:

1. *¿Qué cambios hay ahora con respecto al ejercicio que hace?*
2. *¿Qué cambios hay con respecto a lo que come y cuándo lo come?*
3. *¿Cómo sabemos que el consejo de Susana funciona?*
4. *¿Por qué está tan contenta?*

Exercise 3.17

CD1: 32

¡Escucha!

Escucha el diálogo entre Jorge y el médico, y toma apuntes:

Apuntes:

Nueva dieta de Jorge: . . . .

¿Qué necesita el cuerpo?: . . . .

Ejercicio de Jorge: . . . .

Qué hacer para la espalda: . . . .

Vocabuario
Tirando = so-so, not too bad
El hierro = the iron
Desarrollar = to develop
El músculo = the muscle
Abdominal = abdominal

Exercise 3.18 ✍ 🗩

¡Escribe y luego habla!

Now go back to Exercise 1.7. Choose one of the characters other than the much-maligned Jorge, and write down what you think that particular person's diet consists of.

Vocabulario 3.2

Vocabulario 3.2

A menudo = often
El abdominal = the sit-up
Adelgazar = to lose weight
Cada vez más = more and more
La comida grasa = fatty foods
Desarrollar = to develop
Descansar = to rest
Dicho esto = that said
Disfrutar = to enjoy
En cuanto a = as regards
Engordar = to put on weight
Equilibrado = balanced
El esfuerzo = the effort
En lugar de = instead of
Fijarse en = to take notice of
Funcionar = to work
Hacer ejercicio = to do exercise
Hacer falta = to be necessary
Hacer footing = to go jogging
El hierro = the iron
La imagen = the image, look

Inflarse de comer = to stuff oneself
Ligero = light
Mantenerse en forma = to keep fit
Montar a caballo = to go riding
El músculo = the muscle
Obsesionarse = to become obsessive about
Pesar = to weigh
Ponerse en forma = to get fit
Ponerse a régimen = to go on a diet
Por lo tanto = therefore, consequently
Por supuesto = of course, naturally
Preocuparse = to worry about
Procurar = to try
El punto débil = the weak spot
Reconocer = to admit, recognise
Relajarse = to relax
Super importante = vital
Tener fiebre = to have a temperature
Tirando = so-so, not bad
Tremendo = awful, frightful

Summary of unit

At the end of this unit

You should now be able to: talk about common ailments and symptoms, using a range of expressions; seek advice about remedies; talk, write and understand about aspects of a healthy lifestyle, using new and familiar language from this and previous units.

You might also be able to: work with more complex authentic materials, reading and understanding articles from authentic sources.

About the unit

In this unit you will learn about shopping, in particular shopping for clothes. You will learn about describing clothes and giving opinions and preferences.

New language content:

- expressions of size
- demonstrative adjectives and pronouns (*este, ese, aquel*)
- use of interrogative *¿Cuál?*

New contexts:

- shopping for clothes and presents
- discussion of fashions
- consideration of appropriateness of clothes

La ropa

Although the word 'clothes' is plural in English, the Spanish word, *la ropa* is a singular noun. Therefore, if you were to use *la ropa* with a verb, the verb would also need to be in the singular. Consider this example:

La ropa en esta tienda **es** *muy cara* = the clothes in this shop are very expensive.

Now take a look at the pictures of *Jorge* and *Lucía* below and study the different words:

Las gafas — La gorra — La bufanda — La chaqueta — La camisa — El guante — El cinturón — El pantalón — El calcetín — La zapatilla de deporte

Vocabulario
La gorra = the cap
Las gafas = the glasses
La bufanda = the scarf
La camisa = the shirt
La chaqueta = the coat/jacket
El guante = the glove
El cinturón = the belt
El pantalón = the trousers
El calcetín = the sock
La zapatilla de deporte = the trainer

Vocabulario

El pendiente	=	the earring
La blusa	=	the blouse
El abrigo	=	the overcoat
El paraguas	=	the umbrella
La falda	=	the skirt
Las medias	=	the tights
El zapato	=	the shoe

El paraguas — El pendiente — La blusa — El abrigo — La falda — Las medias — El zapato

CD2: 1

Exercise 4.1

¡Escucha!

1. *Escucha este diálogo entre Julio y su hermano, y toma apuntes abajo.*

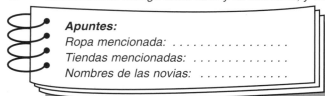

Apuntes:
Ropa mencionada: . . . .
Tiendas mencionadas: . . . .
Nombres de las novias: . . . .

Vocabulario
Regalar = to give as a gift or present
Chulo = cool, trendy
Los grandes almacenes = the department store
Los vaqueros = the jeans
Estar de rebajas = to have a sale on
Una ganga = a bargain
Entré = I went in
Una minifalda = a miniskirt
Mencionar = to mention

Contesta estas preguntas:

1. *¿Por qué Paco dice que un CD es mejor que la ropa?*
2. *¿Por qué le gusta a Julio la tienda en la calle Paz?*
3. *¿Cómo se llaman las novias de Julio y de Paco?*

4.   ¿Qué ropa, en particular, le gusta a la novia de Julio?
5.   ¿Por qué es una buena idea ir a Zara?
6.   ¿Qué va a regalarle Paco a su novia?

Exercise 4.2

¡Lee!

Lee este diálogo entre Julio y una dependienta y luego contesta las preguntas.

Dependienta:	¿Puedo ayudarte?
Julio:	Sí, me gustan mucho estos zapatos. ¿Qué valen?
Dependienta:	¿Cuáles? ¿Estos blancos?
Julio:	No. Estos rojos de aquí.
Dependienta:	Los blancos cuestan menos que los rojos porque están de rebajas, y los rojos no.
Julio:	¿Qué valen?
Dependienta:	Los rojos valen 60 euros, y los blancos, 45.
Julio:	Son un poco caros, ¿no?
Dependienta:	Es una marca muy buena.
Julio:	Y este pantalón de aquí, ¿Qué vale?
Dependienta:	¿Cuál? ¿Éste? ......45 euros. Es otra marca muy buena.
Julio:	Y esta falda negra, ¿Qué vale?
Dependienta:	35 euros, pero no quedan muchas. ¿Para quién es?
Julio:	Para mi novia.
Dependienta:	¿Y qué talla tiene?
Julio:	La 36, creo. No estoy seguro porque solamente salgo con ella desde hace tres semanas.
Dependienta:	Lo siento mucho, pero no quedan de esa talla.
Julio:	Bueno, me llevo los zapatos blancos.
Dependienta:	¿Qué número calza?
Julio:	El 37.
Dependienta:	Muy bien. Ahora mismo te los traigo.

Contesta estas preguntas:

1.   ¿Por qué cuestan menos los zapatos blancos?
2.   ¿Cuánto cuesta el pantalón?
3.   ¿Qué problema hay con la falda negra?
4.   ¿Por qué Julio no está seguro de la talla de su novia?
5.   ¿Qué decide comprar al final?

Vocabulario

Valer = to cost, to be worth
¿Cuál? = which one?
Una marca = a brand, label, make
Quedar = to remain, to be left
La talla = the size
Llevarse = to take (buy)
Calzar = to be of a certain shoe size

Exercise 4.3

¡Escribe y luego habla!

Role-play. Working in pairs and using Exercise 4.2 as a model, invent a dialogue between a shop-assitant and a customer looking for a present for his/her boyfriend/girlfriend. Each person should have at least 5 lines.

¿Cuál?

¿Cuál? is an interrogative pronoun which, as you will have seen from Exercise 4.2, means 'Which one?' Here are the different forms of the pronoun:

Masculine singular	Masculine plural
¿Cuál?	*¿Cuáles?*
Feminine singular	**Feminine plural**
¿Cuál?	*¿Cuáles?*

Este, esta, estos, estas

These words are known as demonstrative adjectives and mean **this** or **these**, depending on whether the noun that follows is singular or plural. Here are the different forms:

Masculine singular	Masculine plural
Este	*Estos*
Feminine singular	**Feminine plural**
Esta	*Estas*

Study these examples:

Quiero comprar este pantalón	=	I want to buy this pair of trousers.
Me gusta esta camisa	=	I like this shirt.
¿Te gustan estos zapatos?	=	Do you like these shoes?
Quiero probarme estas chaquetas	=	I want to try on these jackets.

Exercise 4.4

¡Escribe!

Now write four sentences of your own. As in the examples above, each one should use a different form of the adjective.

Exercise 4.5

¡Escribe!
Usando las palabras de abajo, pon la palabra correcta en cada espacio.

> este   ¿cuáles?   esta   verde   ¿cuál?   estos

Cliente: Quisiera probarme .... camisa.
Dependienta: ¿........? ¿La roja?
Cliente: Sí, y también .... pantalón.
Dependienta: ¿........? ¿El negro?
Cliente: No. El ....Y .... zapatos.
Dependienta: ¿........? ¿Estos de aquí?
Cliente: Sí.

> **Vocabulario**
> *Quisiera* = I would like

Exercise 4.6

¡Escribe!
Traduce este diálogo al español.

A: I would like to try these shoes on.
B: Which ones?
A: These black ones. And this shirt.
B: Which one?
A: This red one.

Exercise 4.7

¡Escribe y luego habla!
Role-play. Working in pairs, invent a further dialogue between customer and shop-assistant. This time, however, you must include one use of *¿Cuál?* and one of *¿Cuáles?* You must also include at least two uses of *este*.

Exercise 4.8

¡Escucha!
Escucha esta conversación telefónica entre Pepe y su amigo inglés Giles y luego contesta las preguntas. Hay que tomar apuntes.

Apuntes:

Llegada de Giles (cómo, cuándo, dónde): ....

Físico de Giles: ....

Ropa de Giles: ....

Ropa de Pepe: ....

Teléfono: ....

> **Vocabulario**
> *Recoger* = to meet, pick up
> *Tener razón* = to be right
> *Ponerse* = to put on (clothes)
> *La mochila* = the rucksack
> *Deberías* = you should
> *El cuero* = the leather
> *De moda* = fashionable, trendy
> *Azul marino* = navy blue
> *El móvil* = the mobile phone
> *Comió* = it ate
> *La agenda* = the phone book
> *¡Buen viaje!* = have a good trip!
> *El anorak* = anorak

Contesta estas preguntas:

1. *¿Cuándo, cómo y adónde llega el amigo de Pepe?*
2. *¿Cómo es físicamente?*
3. *¿Qué ropa va a ponerse?*
4. *¿Por qué tiene que ponerse una chaqueta?*
5. *¿Qué ropa va a ponerse Pepe?*
6. *¿Cuál es el número del móvil de Pepe?*

Exercise 4.9

¡Escribe y luego habla!

Role-play. Working in pairs, and using the dialogue between Pepe and Giles as a model, invent a short conversation between a Spanish boy whose English exchange partner is due to arrive in Spain the following day. Both characters should provide information about what they will be wearing so that the other can recognise him/her. Each character should have at least five lines.

Vocabulario 4.1

Vocabulario 4.1

El abrigo = the coat, overcoat
La agenda = the phonebook
El almacén = the department store
Azul marino = navy blue
La blusa = the blouse
¡Buen viaje! = have a good trip!
La bufanda = the scarf
El calcetín = the sock
Calzar = to be of a certain shoe size
La camisa = the shirt
La chaqueta = the jacket
Chulo = cool
El cinturón = the belt
El cuero = the leather
De moda = fashionable, trendy
Deberías = you should
Estar de rebajas = to be on sale
La falda = the skirt
Las gafas = the glasses
La ganga = the bargain
La gorra = the cap

El guante = the glove
Llevarse = to take (buy)
La marca = the brand
Las medias = the tights, stockings
Mencionar = to mention
La minifalda = the miniskirt
El móvil = the mobile telephone
El pantalón = the pair of trousers
El pendiente = the earring
Ponerse = to put on, wear
Quedar = to be left, to remain
Quisiera = I would like
Recoger = to meet, pick up
Regalar = to give (as a present)
La ropa = the clothes
La talla = the size
Tener razón = to be right
Los vaqueros = the jeans
Valer = to be worth, to cost
El viaje = the journey
Las zapatillas = the trainers

CD2:
6

Exercise 4.10 📖 ✍️

¡Lee!

Lee este diálogo entre un turista y un policía, y luego contesta las preguntas.

Policía:	*Dígame señor.*
Turista:	*Hay unos tipos bastante sospechosos en la playa.*
Policía:	*¿Por qué sospechosos?*
Turista:	*Creo que son ladrones. Están mirando los bolsos y las mochilas de la gente en la playa.*
Policía:	*¿Cuántos son?*
Turista:	*Hay tres.*
Policía:	*¿Y cómo son?*
Turista:	*Hay uno un poco gordo. Lleva un pantalón corto, unas sandalias y una camiseta polo.*
Policía:	*¿De qué color?*
Turista:	*No estoy seguro porque estoy muy nervioso.*
Policía:	*¿Y los otros?*
Turista:	*El segundo lleva un pantalón de chándal, una camiseta y unas zapatillas muy viejas y sucias. El tercero lleva un bañador, una camiseta polo, unas chanclas, y un sombrero. Todos tienen gafas de sol.*
Policía:	*Muy bien. Gracias, señor.*
Turista:	*¿Qué va a hacer?*
Policía:	*Ahora no podemos hacer nada porque ha habido un accidente de tráfico muy grande en la autovía y no puedo mandar a nadie, de momento.*

Contesta estas preguntas:

1. *¿Por qué piensa el turista que los tipos de la playa pueden ser ladrones?*
2. *¿Por qué no está seguro del color de la camiseta polo del primer hombre?*
3. *¿Cómo son las zapatillas del segundo hombre?*
4. *Hay una cosa que llevan todos. ¿Qué es?*
5. *¿Por qué la policía no puede hacer nada de momento?*

Vocabulario

Dígame = how can I help you?
    (literally "tell me")
Un tipo = a person
Sospechoso = suspicious
Un ladrón = a thief
Llevar = to wear
Una sandalia = a sandal
Una camiseta polo = a short-sleeved sports
            shirt
Estoy = I am
Estar seguro = to be sure

Nervioso = nervous, anxious
Una camiseta = a T-shirt
Un chándal = a tracksuit
Un bañador = a swimming costume
Las chanclas = flip-flops
Un sombrero = a hat
Las gafas de sol = the sunglasses
Ha habido = there has been
La autovía = the dual-carriageway
Mandar = to send
De momento = for the time being

Ese, esa, esos, esas

These words are more demonstrative adjectives. Their meaning is **that** or **those**, depending on whether the noun that follows is singular or plural. Here are the different forms categorised according to gender:

Masculine singular	**Masculine plural**
ese	esos
Feminine singular	**Feminine plural**
esa	esas

Study these examples:

Quisiera comprar ese chándal.	= I would like to buy that tracksuit.
Le gusta esa chaqueta.	= He likes that jacket.
¿Qué valen esos zapatos?	= How much are those shoes?
Esas camisas están de moda.	= Those shirts are trendy.

Exercise 4.11

¡Escribe!
Now write 4 sentences of your own. As in the examples, each sentence should use a different form of the adjective.

Exercise 4.12

¡Escribe!
Usando las palabras de abajo, pon la palabra correcta en cada espacio.

> fantásticas   poco   ¿cuál? (x 2)   eres   ese   ¿cuáles?
> esas   esos   moda   esa

Elena:	¿Te gusta .... camisa?
Jorge:	¿.......? ¿La verde?
Elena:	Sí.
Jorge:	No. Pero me gusta .... chándal.
Elena:	¿.......? ¿El negro? Es un .... hortera, ¿no?
Jorge:	No. El negro está muy de ....

Elena:	Y .... zapatos. ¿Te gustan?
Jorge:	No, pero me gustan .... botas.
Elena:	¿.......? ¿Ésas? Son muy feas.
Jorge:	No. Son ....
Elena:	Jorge, ¡que hortera ....!

Exercise 4.13

¡Escribe!
Now translate the dialogue in Exercise 4.12 into English.

> **Vocabulario**
> *Hortera* = tacky
> *La bota* = the boot

Aquel, aquella, aquellos, aquellas

These words are very similar to **_ese, esa, esos, esas_** in that they are also demonstrative adjectives and they mean **that** or **those**. The difference is one of distance. **_Aquel, aquella, aquellos, aquellas_** refer to something that is further away. The implication is therefore **that one** or **those ones <u>over there</u>**. As before, here are the different forms categorised according to gender:

Masculine singular	**Masculine plural**
aquel	*aquellos*
Feminine singular	**Feminine plural**
aquella	*aquellas*

Now study these examples:

Quisiera probarme aquel pantalón.	=	I'd like to try on those trousers.
Me gusta aquella camisa.	=	I like that shirt.
Aquellos zapatos son chulos.	=	Those shoes are cool.
¿Te gustan aquellas camisas?	=	Do you like those shirts?

CD2: 8

Exercise 4.14

¡Escribe!
Now write 4 sentences of your own. As in the examples, each sentence should use a different form of the adjective.

Exercise 4.15

¡Escribe!
See whether you can now redo Exercise 4.12, this time replacing the different forms of **_ese_** with the correct form of **_aquel_**. The other missing words also need to be filled in.

Elena:	¿Te gusta .... camisa?
Jorge:	¿.......? ¿La verde?
Elena:	Sí.
Jorge:	No. Pero me gusta .... chándal.
Elena:	¿.......? ¿El negro? Es un .... hortera, ¿no?
Jorge:	No. El negro está muy de ....
Elena:	Y .... zapatos. ¿Te gustan?
Jorge:	No, pero me gustan .... botas.
Elena:	¿.......? ¿Ésas? Son muy feas.
Jorge:	No. Son ....
Elena:	Jorge, qué hortera ....

Demonstrative pronouns

These words are virtually identical to the demonstrative adjectives that we have looked at before. The only difference is that the pronoun is distinguished from the adjective by an accent. Here are the different forms:

	Singular		Plural	
	Masculine	**Feminine**	**Masculine**	**Feminine**
This one	*éste*	*ésta*	*éstos*	*éstas*
That one (nearer)	*ése*	*ésa*	*ésos*	*ésas*
That one (further away)	*aquél*	*aquélla*	*aquéllos*	*aquéllas*

Exercise 4.16

¡Escribe!

A ver si puedes traducir el diálogo entre Paco y Julio al inglés.

Paco: *¿Qué pantalón te gusta? ¿Éste, ése o aquél?*
Julio: *Me gusta ése. ¿Qué camisa te gusta?*
Paco: *Me gusta aquélla.*
Julio: *¿No prefieres ésta?*
Paco: *No, prefiero aquélla.*

Exercise 4.17

¡Escribe!

Now rewrite the dialogue in Spanish, but substitute *zapatos* for *pantalón* and *camisetas* for *camisa*. Remember that you will need to change the verb *gustar* as well as the demonstrative pronouns.

Esto, eso, aquello

These words are also demonstrative pronouns, but unlike the ones we have just looked at, do not refer to anything specific, unlike the accented forms which refer to specific nouns. They are translated thus:

esto	=	this
eso	=	that (nearer)
aquello	=	that (further away)

Ejemplos:

¿Qué es esto?	=	what is this?
¿Qué es eso?	=	what is that?
¿Qué es aquello?	=	what is that over there?

Exercise 4.18

¡Escucha!
Escucha esta conversación entre Jorge, Elena y una
dependienta y luego contesta las preguntas de abajo.

Contesta estas preguntas:

1. *¿Por qué Elena prefiere la falda verde?*
2. *¿Qué talla tiene Elena?*
3. *¿Por qué no puede probarse la falda que le gusta?*
4. *¿Cómo intenta la dependienta convencer a Elena?*
5. *¿Por qué Elena no quiere probarse el pantalón que le gusta?*
6. *¿Por qué no puede comprar el pantalón?*

Vocabulario
Gracioso = funny
Sentar = to suit
Tener buen tipo = to have a good figure
Un descuento = a discount
Por ciento = per cent
Sentar bien = to fit/suit well
Quedarse = to take, keep
La tarjeta (de crédito) = credit card
En efectivo = by cash
El carné de identidad = the identity card
Convencer = to convince

Exercise 4.19

¡Escribe, y luego habla!
Role-play. Working in pairs, invent a dialogue between a customer and a shop-assistant in a department store. As in the dialogue in Exercise 4.18, the customer has to change his/her mind because the first choice is not available. Each character should have at least 5 lines each.

Exercise 4.20

¡Lee!

Lee esta conversación entre Elena y Angela y luego contesta las preguntas.

Angela:	¿Qué te vas a poner para ir al instituto?
Elena:	No sé, algo cómodo.
Angela:	¿No tienes que llevar uniforme?
Elena:	No, claro que no.
Angela:	¡Qué suerte!
Elena:	¿Estás diciendo que tú tienes que ponerte uniforme?
Angela:	Sí. Tengo que ponerme una falda, unas medias, una chaqueta, e incluso una corbata.
Elena:	¿Y los chicos, también?
Angela:	Sí, claro. Bueno, ellos llevan pantalones en lugar de falda, y calcetines en vez de medias.
Elena:	Normal. Y los profesores, ¿qué ropa llevan?
Angela:	Depende. Los hombres suelen llevar un traje y una corbata, las mujeres una falda o un pantalón y una blusa. ¿Y aquí?
Elena:	Es más informal. Hay algunos profesores que llevan traje, pero muy pocos.
Angela:	Bueno, creo que me voy a poner un pantalón en lugar de una falda.
Elena:	Igual que yo. Dice el pronóstico del tiempo que va a hacer frío.

Contesta estas preguntas:

1. ¿Por qué dice Angela que Elena tiene mucha suerte?
2. ¿Qué diferencias hay entre el uniforme de los chicos y el de las chicas en el colegio de Angela?
3. ¿Por qué las dos chicas van a ponerse un pantalón hoy?

> **Vocabulario**
> El uniforme = the uniform
> E = and (before word beginning in i/hi)
> En lugar de = instead of
> En vez de = instead of
> Normal = natural, normal
> El traje = the suit
> La corbata = the tie
> Igual que yo = me too

Exercise 4.21

¡Escucha!

Escucha este diálogo entre Jorge y su amigo Pedro sobre la ropa que van a ponerse para ir a una discoteca. Luego, contesta las preguntas.

1. ¿Por qué Jorge va a tener problemas para entrar a la discoteca?
2. ¿Qué ropa va a ponerse Pedro?
3. ¿Por qué Pedro no puede prestarle unos vaqueros a Jorge?
4. ¿Por qué Pedro dice que Jorge tiene que volver a casa?
5. ¿Cuánto dinero le da Pedro a Jorge y por qué?
6. ¿Por qué Pedro no puede ir con Jorge a la tienda?
7. ¿Quién es Yolanda?
8. ¿Dónde y cuándo quedan?

Vocabulario

Prestar = to lend
Tener estilo = to be trendy/fashionable
Quedar = to arrange to meet
La dependienta = the shop assistant

Exercise 4.22

¡Lee!

Lee esta conversación entre Julio, Paco y sus padres y luego contesta las preguntas de abajo.

Padre:	Bueno chicos, ¿cuándo os vais a cambiar de ropa? Tenemos la mesa reservada a las diez.
Paco:	¿Por qué no podemos ir así?
Padre:	Porque estáis en pantalones cortos.
Paco:	Pero estoy asado; hace muchísimo calor. Vamos a estar mucho más cómodos así.
Padre:	El restaurante tiene aire acondicionado.
Julio:	¿Es que no vamos a comer fuera?
Padre:	Creo que vamos a estar mejor dentro. Hace mucho calor para estar fuera.
Julio:	Pero hay un jardín enorme fuera y podemos jugar al fútbol.
Padre:	No vamos al restaurante para jugar al fútbol. Vamos a comer.

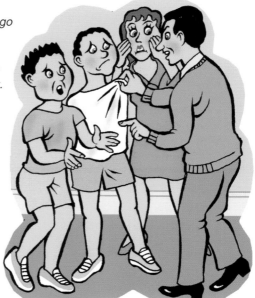

Julio:	*Pero Papá, mañana tenemos un partido muy importante y queremos practicar.*
Padre:	*Lo siento. No puede ser.*
Madre:	*Anda, Jesús, déjalos.*
Padre:	*Que no. Y, como he dicho antes, tenéis que cambiaros de ropa.*
Paco:	*¿Qué me tengo que poner?*
Padre:	*Un pantalón, para empezar.*
Paco:	*¿Mis vaqueros?*
Padre:	*No. Siempre están sucios. Y ponte una camisa limpia y planchada.*
Paco:	*¿Puedo llevar las zapatillas?*
Padre:	*No, no pegan con el pantalón y la camisa. Pónte esos zapatos de cuero que tienes.*
Julio:	*¿Y yo? ¿Qué me pongo?*
Padre:	*Lo mismo que tu hermano.*
Madre:	*¿T tú, Jesús, qué te vas a poner?*
Padre:	*Mi traje nuevo. El dueño del restaurante es un cliente del banco y quiero causar una buena impresión. ¿Y tú?*
Madre:	*Yo me voy a poner ese vestido blanco. Así voy fresquita.*

Contesta estas preguntas:

1. *¿Por qué los chicos tienen que cambiarse de ropa?*
2. *¿Por qué no van a comer fuera?*
3. *¿Qué quieren hacer los chicos en el jardín y por qué?*
4. *¿Por qué Paco no puede llevar vaqueros?*
5. *¿Por qué Paco no puede llevar zapatillas?*
6. *¿Qué ropa va a llevar Julio?*
7. *¿Qué va a ponerse el padre y por qué?*
8. *¿Qué va a ponerse la madre y por qué?*
9. *¿Dónde trabaja el padre?*

Vocabulario

El aire acondicionado = the air-conditioning
Estar asado = to be boiling hot
He dicho = I have said
Planchado = ironed
Pegar con = to go with/suit
La impresión = the impression
El vestido = the dress
El cuero = the leather
Fresquito = cool, fresh
El dueño = the owner

Exercise 4.23

¡Escribe y luego habla!

Role-play. Working in pairs, invent a dialogue between a parent and his/her son/daughter in which the parent expresses displeasure at his/her child's choice of clothes for an occasion of your choice. As in Exercise 4.22, reasons should be given for why the choice is not appropriate and suggestions made as to what clothes should be worn. Equally, the son/daughter should try to justify his/her original choice. Each character should have at least five lines.

Vocabulario 4.2

Vocabulario 4.2

El aire acondicionado = the air-conditioning	*He dicho* = I have said
La autovía = the dual-carriageway	*Hortera* = tacky
El bañador = the swimming-costume	*Igual* = the same, equal
La bota = the boot	*La impresión* = the impression
La camiseta = the T-shirt	*El ladrón* = the thief
La camiseta polo = the short-sleeved sports shirt	*Nervioso* = nervous, anxious
	Normal = normal, natural
El carné de identidad = the I.D. card	*Pegar con* = to suit, go with
El chándal = the tracksuit	*Planchado* = ironed
Convencer = to convince	*Por ciento* = per cent
La corbata = the tie	*Prestar* = to lend
El cuero = the leather	*El pronóstico del tiempo* = the weather forecast
De momento = for the time being	*Quedar* = to arrange to meet
La dependienta = the shop assistant (female)	*Quedarse* = to take, keep (clothes)
El descuento = the discount	*La sandalia* = the sandal
El dueño = the owner	*Sentar* = to suit
En efectivo = by cash	*Sentar bien* = to fit/suit well
En lugar de = instead of	*El sombrero* = the hat
En vez de = instead of	*Sospechoso* = suspicious
Estar asado = to be boiling hot	*La tarjeta de crédito* = the credit card
Estar seguro = to be sure	*Tener buen tipo* = to have a good figure
Fresquito = cool, fresh	*Tener estilo* = to have style, to be fashionable
Las gafas de sol = the sunglasses	*El tipo* = the person
Gracioso = funny	*El traje* = ths suit
Ha habido = there has been	*El uniforme* = the uniform
	El vestido = the dress

Summary of unit

At the end of this unit

You should now be able to: perform role-plays to buy items in shops, stating colour, size and preference, using demonstrative adjectives and pronouns to point out items; describe a choice of clothing for a particular event and say why it is or is not appropriate.

You might also be able to: comprehend, speak and write about more complex situations involving shopping and preferences for clothes.

About the unit

In this unit you will learn to use a range of tenses to talk and write about trips and holidays.

New language content:
- preterite tense of the irregular verb *ir*
- preterite tense or regular *–ar* verbs

New contexts:
- holidays and tourism
- outings and trips
- modes of transport

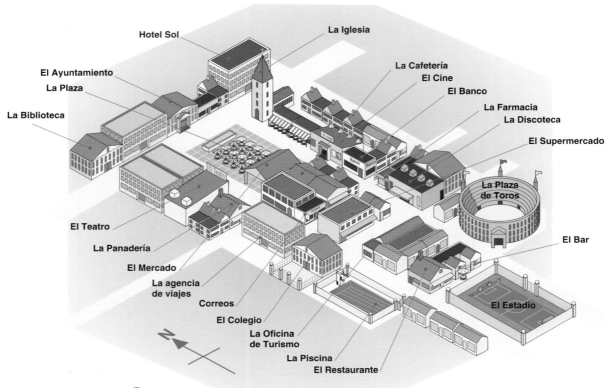

CD2:
14

Exercise 5.1

¡Escucha!

Escucha esta conversación entre Pedro y Elena. Toma apuntes abajo y luego contesta las preguntas.

Apuntes:

¿Adónde van ahora?: . . . .

¿Qué países quieren visitar?: . . . .

¿Por qué?: . . . .

¿Cuándo/Por qué?: . . . .

¿Idea de Elena al final?: . . . .

Contesta estas preguntas:

1. *¿Adónde va Elena y por qué?*
2. *¿Qué país quiere visitar y por qué?*
3. *¿Cuándo quiere viajar y por qué?*
4. *¿Adónde va Pedro y por qué?*
5. *¿Qué país quiere visitar y por qué?*
6. *¿Cuándo quiere viajar y por qué?*
7. *¿Adónde van a ir antes de ir a Correos y a la agencia?*

Exercise 5.2

¡Escribe y luego habla!

Role-play. Working in pairs, invent a conversation between two friends who meet on the street, each on their way to a different location in the city centre. In the course of the dialogue both characters should make clear where they are going and why.

Exercise 5.3

¡Lee!

Lee esta conversación entre Carmen y su amiga Rosa y luego contesta las preguntas.

Carmen: Entonces, ¿qué planes tienes para el verano?

Rosa: Todavía no estoy segura. Depende de mi trabajo en la tienda. Si tengo dinero suficiente me gustaría ir al extranjero, pero si no, supongo que iré a la playa con mis padres. ¿Y tú?

Carmen: Bueno, mi amiga inglesa Poppy me ha invitado a su casa en Londres, pero ya conozco Inglaterra un poco y tengo ganas de ir a otro sitio.

Rosa: ¿Dónde por ejemplo?

Carmen: No sé. Los Estados Unidos, Australia, La India, un país exótico así. El problema es que no me gusta mucho volar. Además, va a costar mucho. Entonces pienso que no va a ser posible.

Rosa: ¿Y por qué no vas a un país más cercano como Francia o Italia?

Carmen: No hablo francés y me han dicho que eso puede ser un problema. Italia, la conozco ya. Una de las hermanas de mi madre está casada con un italiano y vive en Roma. He ido a verlos varias veces. Y tú, si tienes dinero, ¿adónde vas a ir?

Rosa: Me gustaría mucho conocer Irlanda. Yo no aguanto el calor, y creo que nunca hace calor en Irlanda. Además, me han dicho que la gente es muy simpática. También, la cerveza irlandesa me encanta, sobre todo la "Guinness".

Vocabulario

Al extranjero = abroad
Iré = I will go
Ha invitado = has invited
Tener ganas de = to want to, feel like
Exótico = exotic
Volar = to fly
Cercano = near
Casado = married
He ido = I've gone
Aguantar = to put up with, stand, tolerate

Contesta estas preguntas:

1. *¿Por qué Rosa no está segura de sus planes para el verano?*
2. *¿Por qué Carmen no quiere ir a Inglaterra?*
3. *¿Por qué Carmen piensa que no le va a ser posible ir a un país exótico?*
4. *¿Por qué tampoco quiere ir a Francia o Italia?*
5. *¿Por qué está su tía en Italia?*
6. *¿Adónde quiere ir Rosa y por qué?*

Exercise 5.4

¡Escribe y luego habla!

Role-play. Working in pairs, invent a dialogue between two friends discussing their plans for the summer holidays. As in Exercise 5.3, you should each state where you would ideally like to go, but also provide a reason why you cannot do so. You should then provide an alternative and explain what it is that you like about that particular country.

Exercise 5.5

CD2: 16

¡Escucha!

Escucha esta conversación entre Paco, Julio y sus padres sobre las vacaciones. Toma apuntes abajo para luego contestar las preguntas.

> **Vocabulario**
> *Estarán* = they will be
> *Los tuyos* = yours
> *Jugar al dominó* = to play dominoes
> *El esquí acuático* = water-skiing
> *La barca* = the boat
> *Ninguna parte* = nowhere
> *La estación de esquí* = the ski resort
> *Hemos esquiado* = we have skied
> *Veranear* = to spend the summer holidays
> *Ya veremos* = we will see

Apuntes:	País/región	Por qué/actividades	Cuando
Paco:	. . . .	. . . .	. . . .
Julio:	. . . .	. . . .	. . . .
Padre:	. . . .	. . . .	. . . .
Madre:	. . . .	. . . .	. . . .

Contesta estas preguntas:

1.   *¿Adónde quiere ir el padre y cuándo?*
2.   *¿Por qué quiere ir allí y qué se puede hacer en ese sitio?*
3.   *¿Adónde quiere ir Paco, cuándo y por qué?*
4.   *¿Qué prefiere Julio?*
5.   *¿Cuándo quiere ir de vacaciones y por qué?*
6.   *¿Por qué no le gusta esta idea a Paco?*
7.   *¿Qué prefiere la madre y por qué?*

Exercise 5.6 📖 ✍️

¡Lee!
*Lee este diálogo entre el padre de Julio y Paco y el agente de
una agencia de viajes y luego contesta las preguntas.*

Agente:	*Buenos días.*
Padre:	*Buenos días.*
Agente:	*¿Cómo puedo ayudarle?*
Padre:	*Necesito infomación sobre estaciones de esquí.*
Agente:	*Vale. ¿En este país o en el extranjero?*
Padre:	*En el extranjero.*
Agente:	*¿Qué países le interesan?*
Padre:	*Los más baratos.*
Agente:	*¿Cuándo quiere ir?*
Padre:	*En Navidad. Después de Nochebuena. No podemos ir antes porque vienen mis suegros a quedarse con nosotros. No se van hasta el 28 de diciembre.*
Agente:	*¿Cuántas personas?*
Padre:	*Cuatro. Mi mujer y yo y nuestros dos hijos.*
Agente:	*¿Qué edad tienen?*
Padre:	*Dieciséis y dieciocho lañes.*
Agente:	*¿Cuánto tiempo quieren estar?*
Padre:	*No estoy seguro; depende del precio.*

Contesta estas preguntas:

1.   *¿Por qué está el padre de Julio y Paco en la agencia de viajes?*
2.   *¿Por qué la familia no puede ir hasta después de Nochebuena?*
3.   *¿Por qué no sabe cuánto tiempo quiere estar?*

> **Vocabulario**
> *Los suegros* = in-laws

Exercise 5.7 ✍️

In Exercise 5.6 there are several examples of interrogative pronouns. These are question words such as *¿Qué?*, *¿Cómo?* Now go back through the dialogue in Exercise 5.6 and write down all the different examples of interrogative pronouns.

Exercise 5.8 ✍ 💬

¡Escribe!

Role-play. Working in pairs, write a conclusion to the dialogue in Exercise 5.6. Both *Padre* and the *agente de viajes* should have at least three lines each.

Exercise 5.9 ✍

¡Escribe!

Using the *usted* form, translate the following sentences into Spanish:

1. How do you want to travel?
2. When do you want to go?
3. How long do you want to stay?
4. What countries do you like?
5. How much money can you spend?

Exercise 5.10 ✍ 💬

¡Escribe!

Role-play. Working in pairs, write a new dialogue between a client and a travel agent. The travel agent should try to use as many different interrogative pronouns as possible, and the client should answer appropriately. Each character should have at least six lines each.

Exercise 5.11 📖 ✍

¡Lee y escribe!

Lee la carta de Elena a su amiga inglesa y luego decide si las frases de después son correctas o falsas. Si son verdaderas, pon una V al lado. Si son falsas, escribe 'falsa' y luego escribe la frase correcta.

Querida Poppy:

¿Qué tal? Yo estoy muy bien pero un poco nerviosa. Es mi madre. Me hace mil preguntas cada día sobre el viaje. Es tan pesada. Ya tengo mi billete. Salgo el seis de julio. No puedo ir antes porque a lo mejor tengo que repetir unos exámenes. Tengo que coger el vuelo que sale por la tarde porque así mi padre me puede llevar a Málaga en el "Seat". Llego a las diez y media. ¿Tú me puedes recoger? Espero que sí porque yo no sé llegar a tu casa. Bueno, ¿qué vamos a hacer durante las vacaciones? ¿Vamos a ir a Escocia? Espero que sí. Me encantaría volver a ir al festival de Edimburgo. ¿Cuánto tiempo vamos a estar allí? ¿Qué más vamos a hacer? Y tú, ¿qué tal? ¿Cómo va el colegio? Aquí estamos en la época de los exámenes, así que tengo bastante trabajo. Bueno, tengo que irme. A ver si me contestas pronto.

Un abrazo fuerte.

Elena

1. *Elena está nerviosa a causa del viaje.*
2. *Va en avión.*
3. *Va sola a Málaga.*
4. *Va a Málaga en tren.*
5. *Llega a las diez y media de la noche.*
6. *No conoce Escocia.*
7. *Tiene mucho trabajo.*

CD2: 18

Exercise 5.12

¡Escucha!
Escucha esta conversación entre Jorge y Elena y luego contesta las preguntas de abajo.

Vocabulario

1. *¿Cuál es el 'problema' de Elena?*
2. *¿Cuál es la 'idea' de Jorge?*
3. *¿Por qué no puede ir Jorge?*
4. *¿Cuánto tiempo va a estar Elena en las Islas Británicas?*
5. *¿Por qué Elena va en avión?*
6. *¿Cuándo vuelve Elena a España?*

Vocabulario

No seas tonta = Don't be silly
No sabía nada = I didn't know anything
   (about it)
¡Ni hablar! = no way!

CD2: 19

Exercise 5.13

¡Lee!
Lee y estudia el diálogo de abajo.

Eva:	*Hola Juan, ¿adónde vas?*
Juan:	*Hola. Voy a Almería, ¿y tú?*
Eva:	*Voy a Madrid. ¿Cómo vas?*
Juan:	*En autocar, ¿y tú?*
Eva:	*En tren.*
Juan:	*¡Que lo pases bien!*

Exercise 5.14

¡Escribe y, luego, habla!

Role-play. Working in pairs, and using the dialogue in Exercise 5.13 as your model, invent a brief dialogue between two friends talking about where they are going and how they are going to get there. Choose between the modes of transport and locations on the map below. As in Exercise 5.13, each person should have three lines.

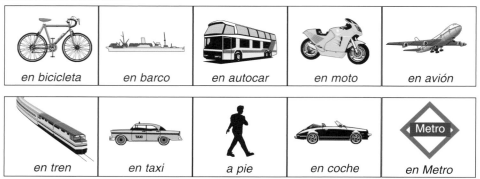

| en bicicleta | en barco | en autocar | en moto | en avión |
| en tren | en taxi | a pie | en coche | en Metro |

The future: revision

The simplest way to express plans for the future is to use the following formula:

Ir + *a* + infinitive

Study these examples:

Voy a comprar el periódico luego	=	I'm going to buy the paper later.
Juan va a ver a su madre el martes	=	Juan is going to see his mother on Tuesday.
Vamos a ir a Francia este verano	=	We're going to go to France this summer.

Exercise 5.15 ✍️

¡Escribe!

Complete the sentences below by using the appropriate part of *ir* as well as a suitable infinitive:

1. *Nosotros .... a .... en el restaurante.*
2. *Mi madre .... a .... a Madrid en coche.*
3. *¿Tú .... a .... la película esta noche?*
4. *¿Vosotros .... a .... los deberes hoy o mañana?*
5. *Yo .... a .... el sol en la playa.*

Exercise 5.16 ✍️

¡Escribe!

Now invent five future sentences of your own, each using a different part of *ir* and a different infinitive.

The preterite tense and the verb ir

The **preterite** tense, as we will see further shortly, is of fundamental importance when it comes to describing events and actions in the past that are finite. In other words, it is normally the tense to use when describing something that is over and done with. E.g. 'I went to Spain last year.' As the example illustrates, the verb *ir* is also vital when describing trips and holidays. So, let's look at how the irregular verb *ir* works in the **preterite**:

fui	= I went		*fuimos*	= we went
fuiste	= you went		*fuisteis*	= you went
fue	= he went		*fueron*	= they went

Exercise 5.17 ✍️

¡Escribe!

Traduce las frases de abajo al español:

1. He went to France last summer.
2. We went to the shops yesterday.
3. They went to Italy to ski.
4. I went to the beach to sunbathe.
5. Did you (sing) go to Greece?
6. Did you (plural) go to Scotland?

Exercise 5.18

¡Escribe!

Using the pictures below, invent five sentences using *ir* in the preterite. Try to use different parts of the verb. Look at these examples:

Jorge fue a Escocia para ver a Elena = Jorge went to Scotland to see Elena.
Fui a la playa para tomar el sol = I went to the beach to sunbathe.

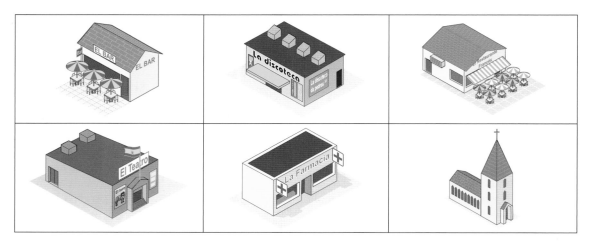

Exercise 5.19

¡Escucha!

Escucha esta conversación entre Poppy y Elena sobre sus vacaciones. Toma apuntes abajo para luego contestar las preguntas:

Apuntes:	Elena:	Poppy:
Normalmente:	. . . .	. . . .
El verano pasado:	. . . .	. . . .
El futuro:	. . . .	. . . .

Contesta estas preguntas:

1. *¿Qué significa la palabra 'veranear'?*
2. *¿Dónde veranea Elena normalmente y por qué?*
3. *¿Dónde veranea Poppy normalmente y por qué?*
4. *¿Por qué no le gusta?*
5. *¿Adónde fue Poppy el verano pasado y por qué?*
6. *¿Adónde fue Elena y qué tal?*
7. *¿Adónde quieren ir en el futuro?*

Exercise 5.20

¡Lee!

Lee esta conversación entre Jorge y Manolo y luego contesta las preguntas.

Manolo:	Hola Jorge. ¿Qué tal? Fui a tu casa ayer, pero no estabas.
Jorge:	No, fui a la agencia de viajes.
Manolo:	¿Por qué?
Jorge:	Voy a ir a Escocia en julio para ver a Elena.
Manolo:	Qué bien, ¿no?
Jorge:	Espero que sí. Va a ser una sorpresa.
Manolo:	¿Fuiste al concierto por la noche?
Jorge:	No. Fui al supermercado. Vamos a hacer una barbacoa este fin de semana. Y tú, ¿fuiste al bar con esa chica?
Manolo:	Sí fuimos, pero estaba cerrado, así que fuimos a ver una película. Entonces, ¿vas a ir a Escocia? ¿Qué vas a hacer allí?
Jorge:	Pues primero, comprarme un paraguas. Dicen que llueve mucho allí.
Manolo:	Sí, pero eso está bien. Todo está muy verde; es precioso.
Jorge:	¿Lo conoces?
Manolo:	Sí. Fui con mi hermano hace dos años. ¡Qué maravilla!

Contesta estas preguntas:

1. ¿Por qué Jorge no estaba en su casa ayer?
2. Elena sabe que va a ir a Escocia. ¿Verdad o mentira?
3. ¿Por qué Jorge no fue al concierto?
4. ¿Adónde fue Manolo, y con quién?
5. ¿Por qué todo está muy verde en Escocia?

> **Vocabulario**
> No estabas = you weren't there
> Mejorar = to improve, get better
> El campeonato = the championship
> El motociclismo = motorcycling
> ¡Qué rollo! = what a pain/bore!

Exercise 5.21

¡Escucha y luego habla!

Escucha a Carlos, Eva y Nuria sobre dónde fueron la semana pasada. Toma apuntes para luego contestar las preguntas del profesor/la profesora.

Apuntes:	Carlos	Eva	Nuria
¿Dónde?	. . . .	. . . .	. . . .
¿Con quién?	. . . .	. . . .	. . . .
¿Por qué?	. . . .	. . . .	. . . .

The preterite tense and -ar verbs

We have already met the preterite tense of the verb *ir*. As you know, this tense is used to describe an action which happened in the past and is now complete.

The rule for regular *-ar* verbs in the preterite is that you remove the *-ar* ending and add the following endings:

-é	*-amos*
-aste	*-asteis*
-ó	*-aron*

So, if we consider a verb such as *hablar*, we end up with:

hablé	*hablamos*
hablaste	*hablasteis*
habló	*hablaron*

This then gives us the meanings:
I spoke
You spoke
He/she spoke, etc.

Exercise 5.22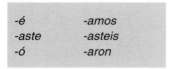

¡Escribe!
Using the rule given above, write out the following verbs in the preterite tense:

1. *Comprar*
2. *Viajar*
3. *Bailar*

Exercise 5.23

¡Escribe!
Traduce estas frases al español:

1. We travelled to Spain by plane.
2. He bought a new car yesterday.
3. What did you (sing.) buy at the shops?
4. Last night they danced with two beautiful girls.
5. He travelled to Scotland to see his girlfriend.
6. I danced until 2 o'clock.
7. Did you (sing.) travel by train?
8. Did you (plural) dance with those women?
9. They bought lots of meat.
10. I travelled to Spain by boat.

Exercise 5.24

¡Escucha!

Listen to this conversation between Carlos, Eva and Nuria. Then copy and complete the table below. For each of the three characters, you need to answer the following questions:

1.   *¿Adónde fue?*
2.   *¿Cómo fue?*
3.   *¿Qué tal lo pasó?*
4.   *¿Qué hizo?*

> **Vocabulario**
> *No había* = there wasn't
> *Estaba* = it was
> *Estropeado* = broken

Exercise 5.25

¡Escribe y luego habla!

Role-play. Working in pairs, invent a brief conversation between two friends talking about what they did in the holidays. You should include information about where you went, how, whether or not you enjoyed yourself, and what you did. You should aim to use the preterite tense of *ir* and regular *–ar* verbs.

Exercise 5.26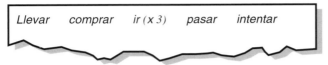

¡Lee!

Read the e-mail below and then, choosing from the verbs below, insert the correct verb in the correct tense in each gap.

> Llevar   comprar   ir *(x 3)*   pasar   intentar

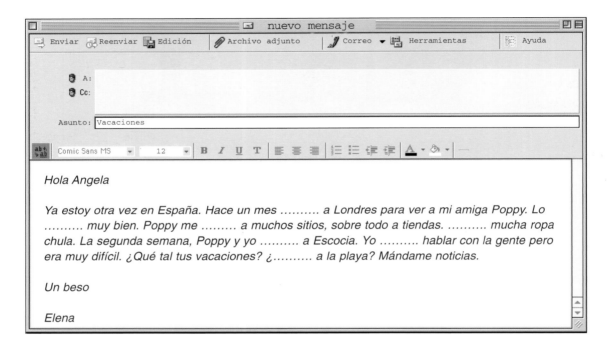

nuevo mensaje

Enviar   Reenviar   Edición   Archivo adjunto   Correo ▾   Herramientas   Ayuda

A:
Cc:
Asunto: Vacaciones

Comic Sans MS ▾ 12 ▾ **B** *I* <u>U</u> T

Hola Angela

Ya estoy otra vez en España. Hace un mes .... a Londres para ver a mi amiga Poppy. Lo .... muy bien. Poppy me .... a muchos sitios, sobre todo a tiendas. .... mucha ropa chula. La segunda semana, Poppy y yo .... a Escocia. Yo .... hablar con la gente pero era muy difícil. ¿Qué tal tus vacaciones? ¿.......... a la playa? Mándame noticias.

Un beso

Elena

Exercise 5.27

¡Escribe!

Using *ir* and regular *-ar* verbs, write a short reply to Elena, stating where you went during your holidays and telling her what you did.

Reflexive regular -ar verbs in the preterite

The rule for these verbs is exactly the same as for normal *-ar* verbs, with the exception that the appropriate reflexive pronoun has to be put before the verb. Let's consider the verb *acostarse*:

Yo **me acosté**	Nosotros **nos acostamos**
Tú **te acostaste**	Vosotros **os acostasteis**
Él **se acostó**	Ellos **se acostaron**

N.B. You will see that, although *acostarse* (*ue*) is a radical-changing verb, there is no vowel change in radical-changing *-ar* verbs in the preterite tense.

Exercise 5.28

¡Escribe!

Now see whether you can write out the correct forms of the following verbs in the preterite.

1. *Levantarse*
2. *Bañarse*

Exercise 5.29

CD2:
24

¡Escribe!

Using the words below, create a story of you own invention of between 60 and 100 words. The verbs should be used in the preterite tense. Clearly, you can add other words of your own choice, but, as far as the verbs are concerned, you can only use *–ir* and regular *–ar* verbs:

ir	*levantarse*	*bañarse*	*el hombre gordo*	*mucho*
bailar	*una chica guapísima*	*rápido*	*la playa*	
el sábado				

Exercise 5.30

¡Lee!

Read this conversation between *Jorge* and *Manolo* and underline all the examples of the preterite tense.

Manolo:	*Hola Jorge. ¿Qué tal lo pasaste en Escocia?*
Jorge:	*Regular. Elena estaba enfadadísima. No me habló.*
Manolo:	*¿Qué?*
Jorge:	*Bueno, me habló, pero solamente para llamarme gordo, asqueroso y feo.*
Manolo:	*¡Qué injusto! No eres ni asqueroso ni feo.*
Jorge:	*¡Qué gracioso!*
Manolo:	*Lo siento. ¿Te quedaste con ella y su amiga?*
Jorge:	*No. No me dejaron. Me quedé en un parque, en un banco.*
Manolo:	*¿Con o sin jacuzzi?*
Jorge:	*¡Muy divertido! Y tú, ¿qué tal?*
Manolo:	*Fui a la playa. Me quedé con mi abuela.*
Jorge:	*¿Qué tal lo pasaste?*
Manolo:	*Lo pasé mejor que tú, seguro.*

Vocabulario
Enfadado = angry
Asqueroso = disgusting
Injusto = unjust
El banco = the bench

Exercise 5.31 ✎

¡Escribe!
Traduce el diálogo de Exercise 5.30 entre Jorge y Manolo al inglés.

Vocabulario 5.1

For this unit we are being generous and only giving you one vocabulary to learn.

Vocabulario 5.1

La agencia de viajes = the travel agents	*La estación de esquí* = the ski resort
Aguantar = to put up with, stand, tolerate	*Estropeado* = broken
Al extranjero = abroad	*Exótico* = exotic
Asqueroso = disgusting	*Injusto* – unjust
El banco = the bench	*Ninguna parte* = nowhere
La barca = the boat	*No había* = there wasn't
Cercano = near	*No seas tonta* = don't be silly
Correos = the Post Office	*Los suegros* = the parents-in-law
El detalle = the detail	*Un paraguas* = an umbrella
Enfadado = angry	*Tener ganas de* = to want to
La época = the period, time	*Tuyo* = yours
El esquí acuático = water-skiing	*Veranear* = to spend the summer holidays
Estaba = it was	*Volar* = to fly

Summary of unit

At the end of this unit

You should now be able to: understand information about transport, outings and holidays; take part in conversations about plans for the weekend and holidays; describe a holiday or an outing in the preterite tense (using ir and regular –ar verbs), detailing where you went, how you travelled, and, to some extent, what you did; read and comprehend texts about holidays, deducing meanings and using a dictionary where necessary.

About the unit

In this unit you will learn to talk and write about a variety of events in the past. You will consolidate your knowledge of the preterite tense.

New language content:

- all forms of the preterite tense of regular *–er* and *–ir* verbs, e.g. *comer*, *salir* and irregular verbs such as *hacer*, *ver*, *estar*
- certain uses of the imperfect tense

New contexts:

- entertainment
- concerts, cinema, theatre, sport, a bullfight
- ordering and buying tickets
- describing a past event or an outing

Exercise 6.1

CD2: 25

¡Lee!

Lee esta conversación telefónica entre Jorge y Manolo y luego contesta las preguntas.

Manolo: Dígame.

Jorge: Hola. Soy Jorge.

Manolo: Hola Jorge. ¿Qué tal?

Jorge: Fatal. Después de todo este tiempo, Elena todavía no me habla. La llamo todos los días pero su madre dice que no quiere hablar conmigo. Estoy hecho polvo. ¿Podemos hacer algo juntos?

Manolo: Claro, hombre. ¿Qué te apetece?

Jorge: No sé, cualquier cosa.

Manolo: ¿Te apetece ir al cine, por ejemplo?

Jorge: No mucho. Fui ayer con mis padres.

Manolo: ¿Quieres ir al concierto de "Ketama"?

Jorge: Me encantaría. Los vi hace dos años y fue fantástico. ¿Cuándo es?

Manolo: Mañana.

Jorge: Pero va a ser imposible conseguir entradas.

Manolo: No te preocupes. Tengo enchufe. Tengo un amigo que conoce al grupo muy bien. Él me puede conseguir entradas, seguro.

Jorge: Pues sí, tío. Sería un punto. ¿Dónde quedamos?

Manolo: No sé. Tocan en la plaza de toros. Podemos quedar allí o, como yo voy en moto, te puedo recoger y podemos ir juntos.

Jorge: Vale. Estupendo.

Manolo: Te veo en tu casa a eso de las nueve. Si hay algún problema te llamo, ¿vale?

Jorge: Vale. Hasta luego, y muchas gracias.

Manolo: De nada, hombre. Hasta mañana.

> **Vocabulario**
>
> *Estar hecho polvo* = to be distraught/extremely tired
> *Conseguir* = to get
> *La entrada* = the ticket (for cinema, concert etc)
> *Tener enchufe* = to have contacts
> *El grupo* = the group, band
> *Ser un punto* = to be great

Contesta estas preguntas en inglés:

1. Why is Jorge feeling so awful?
2. Why does he not want to go to the cinema?
3. Why is he particularly keen to go to the concert?
4. What reason does Manolo give for being confident that he can get tickets?
5. Where is the concert taking place?
6. How are they both going to go to the concert?

Exercise 6.2 ✍️

¡Escribe!

Traduce la conversación de abajo al español.

Carlos:	Do you feel like going out tonight?
Ana:	I'd love to. Where do you want to go to?
Carlos:	Shall we go to the cinema?
Ana:	What are they showing?
Carlos:	The new Almodóvar film.
Ana:	Fantastic. At what time does it start?
Carlos:	There's a showing at 8.30.
Ana:	OK. Where shall we meet, and at what time?
Carlos:	At 8.15 at the box-office.
Ana:	OK. See you later.

Vocabulario

Apetecer	=	to feel like
Poner	=	to show a film
Una sesión	=	a showing/screening
Quedar	=	to arrange to meet
La taquilla	=	the box-office

Exercise 6.3 ✍️ 🗨️

¡Escribe y luego habla!

Role-play. Using the dialogue in Exercise 6.2 as a model, and choosing from the pictures below, invent a dialogue between two friends making plans to go out for the evening. Each person should have at least five lines.

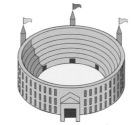

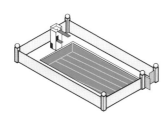

The preterite tense of regular –er and –ir verbs

The preterite tense or regular *–er* and *–ir* verbs is formed by removing the *–er* and *–ir* from the infinitive and adding the following endings:

-í	*-imos*
-iste	*-isteis*
-ió	*-ieron*

Study the following examples:

comer				**vivir**			
Yo	comí	Nosotros	comimos	Yo	viví	Nosotros	vivimos
Tú	comiste	Vosotros	comisteis	Tú	viviste	Vosotros	vivisteis
Él	comió	Ellos	comieron	Él	vivió	Ellos	vivieron

Exercise 6.4

¡Escribe!
Write out the correct forms of the preterite of the verbs below:

1. *volver*
2. *salir*

Exercise 6.5

¡Escribe!
Traduce las frases de abajo al español.

1. I ate lots of prawns yesterday.
2. He returned to Spain without his girlfriend.
3. 'When did you (sing.) return?' his mother asked.
4. We went out after having dinner.
5. I went out with a very beautiful girl last night.

Exercise 6.6

CD2: 27

¡Escucha!
Escucha esta conversación telefónica entre Carlos y Nuria y luego contesta las preguntas de abajo en inglés.

1. Why is Nuria uncertain about whether she should go out or not?
2. Why is she a little reluctant to agree to Carlos' subsequent suggestion?
3. How does Carlos try to persuade her?
4. Why does Carlos suggest they meet in the bar in the Hotel Reina Cristina?
5. Why can Nuria not go by moped?
6. Why does she not want to go by bus?
7. How does she decide to go in the end?
8. Why is Carlos unable to meet before 9.30?

> **Vocabulario**
> *Las procesiones* = the Easter week holy processions
> *Emocionante* = exciting
> *Céntrico* = central
> *El taller* = the garage/mechanics
> *Además* = besides

Exercise 6.7

¡Lee!

Lee esta conversación entre Jorge y Pedro y luego usando la lista de abajo, rellena los espacios con la palabra adecuada.

sé	llena	contigo	taquilla	fui	conmigo
suerte	dónde	entradas	llamo	quedamos	amigo
conoce	corrida	ambiente	quiero	crees	

Pedro: Hola Jorge, ¿qué tal?

Jorge: Fenomenal. Ayer .... al concierto de Ketama.

Pedro: ¡Qué ....! ¿Cómo conseguiste ....?

Jorge: Mi .... Manolo .... al grupo.

Pedro: ¿........ tocaron?

Jorge: En la plaza de toros. Estaba .... y había un .... increíble.

Pedro: Yo .... ir a la plaza de toros el sábado. Va a haber una .... muy buena.

Jorge: Yo voy .... si quieres. ¿Qué toreros van a torear?

Pedro: El Juli, Fran Rivera y Enrique Ponce.

Jorge: ¿Tú .... que va a haber entradas?

Pedro: No .... Pero mañana voy a la .... para ver si todavía quedan. ¿Quieres venir ....?

Jorge: Vale. Te .... por la mañana para decirte donde ....

> **Vocabulario**
> Lleno = full
> La taquilla = the ticket-office/box-office
> El ambiente = the atmosphere

Exercise 6.8

¡Escucha!

Escucha esta conversación telefónica entre Jorge y Pedro y luego contesta las preguntas de abajo en español.

1. ¿Por qué no tienen que ir a la taquilla?
2. ¿Cuánto cuestan las entradas?
3. ¿Para qué parte de la plaza son las entradas?
4. ¿Cuándo empieza la corrida?
5. ¿Por qué van a quedar antes?
6. ¿Cómo van a ir a la plaza?

> **Vocabulario**
> A la sombra = in the shade

PLAZA DE TOROS

CD2:
30

Exercise 6.9

¡Escucha!

*Escucha este diálogo entre Carlos, Nuria y Eva,
y toma apuntes para luego contestar las preguntas.*

Apuntes

Título de la película: . . . .

Cine: . . . .

Sala: . . . .

Sesión: . . . .

Precio de la entrada: . . . .

Otros: . . . .

Vocabulario
Obsesionado = obsessed
Darse cuenta de = to realise
El actor = the actor
La sala = the screen number
Me da igual = it's all the same to me
Invitar = to pay for someone else
El título = the title

Exercise 6.10

¡Lee!

Lee esta carta de Jorge a Elena y luego contesta, en inglés, las preguntas de abajo.

Querida Elena:

Te estoy escribiendo esta carta puesto que no contestas mis llamadas. Estoy muy triste y me gustaría poder hablar contigo. Como sabes, siento mucho lo de Escocia.

Bueno, te cuento un poco lo que he hecho últimamente: el otro día salí con Manolo. Fuimos al concierto de "Ketama". Lo pasamos bomba. Fuimos en la moto de Manolo. Primero, comimos unas tapas en ese bar que a ti te gusta, al lado de la plaza de toros. Luego, entramos en la plaza, a eso de las diez, pero la banda no empezó a tocar hasta las doce porque había unos problemas con el sonido y tardaron mucho en solucionarlos. Pero mereció la pena. ¡Qué maravilla!

Luego, el sábado, fui a una corrida con Pedro. No me costó nada porque su padre nos invitó. ¡Qué suerte!

¿Por qué no me cuentas lo que tú has hecho y a ver si podemos vernos otra vez?

Te echo mucho de menos.

Un beso muy fuerte.

Jorge

Vocabulario
La llamada = the call (telephone)
Sentir = to be sorry about
Lo de = the business about
Había = there was/there were
Tardar = to take time to do something
El sonido = the sound
Merecer la pena = to be worthwhile
Has hecho = you have done
Echar de menos = to miss

Contesta estas preguntas en inglés:

1. Why is Jorge writing to Elena?
2. What did Jorge and Manolo do before going into the bullring?
3. Why did the band not start playing until midnight?
4. What does Jorge say about his trip to the bullfight?

Exercise 6.11

¡Lee!
Lee la carta otra vez y subraya todos los ejemplos del pretérito.

Exercise 6.12

¡Escribe!
Using verbs that are regular in the preterite tense, write a letter to a friend describing what you did last week. You should use at least eight different verbs and write between 80 – 100 words in total.

Exercise 6.13

¡Lee!
Read this diary entry of *Elena* and then rewrite the text, replacing all the verbs in the present tense with their correct forms in the preterite:

Hoy voy al buzón. Encuentro una carta de Jorge. Me pide perdón, pero solamente habla de sí mismo. Cuenta que sale con su amigo, que come tapas, que lo pasa bomba. ¡Qué egoísta!

Exercise 6.14

¡Escribe!
Using the preterite tense of verbs that are regular in the preterite, write a short diary account of what you did one day earlier this week. You should write 25-30 words.

The preterite tense of hacer, ver, estar y decir

As usual with Spanish grammar, just to make sure we don't get too comfortable, there are a number of irregularities, and this applies to the preterite tense. Let's take a look at four important irregular verbs.

Hacer

Yo	hice	Nosotros	hicimos
Tú	hiciste	Vosotros	hicisteis
Él	hizo	Ellos	hicieron

Ver

Yo	vi	Nosotros	vimos
Tú	viste	Vosotros	visteis
Él	vio	Ellos	vieron

Estar

Yo	estuve	Nosotros	estuvimos
Tú	estuviste	Vosotros	estuvisteis
Él	estuvo	Ellos	estuvieron

Decir

Yo	dije	Nosotros	dijimos
Tú	dijiste	Vosotros	dijisteis
Él	dijo	Ellos	dijeron

Exercise 6.15

¡Escribe!
Pon la palabra adecuada en las frases de abajo.

1. *Julio .... (ver) que su madre estaba enfadada e .... (hacer) sus deberes muy rápido.*
2. *Juan .... (estar) en Alemania el año pasado.*
3. *Ana y Carlos .... (ver) una película estupenda el sábado.*
4. *Nosotros .... (ver) a nuestra abuela la semana pasada.*
5. *Yo .... (hacer) todo lo posible para conseguir entradas.*
6. *Ella .... (decir) que sí.*

Exercise 6.16

¡Escribe!
Traduce las frases en Exercise 6.15 al inglés.

Exercise 6.17

CD2: 31

¡Escribe!
Usando las palabras de abajo, pon la palabra adecuada en su sitio.

empezó	volvió	pagó	hizo	cenaron	dijo
preguntó	terminó	salió	salieron	fue	fueron
vio	invitó				

Carlos .... sus deberes lo más rápido posible. .... de su casa a las ocho y .... a su bar favorito. Allí .... a Ana. Le .... si quería ir al cine. Ella .... que sí. Carlos .... al camarero y los dos .... del bar y .... directamente al cine. Como Ana no tenía dinero, Carlos la .... La película .... a las ocho y media y .... a las diez. Después, ... en un restaurante chino. Carlos .... a casa a las once y media.

Exercise 6.18

¡Escucha!
Escucha a Julio hablando de sus vacaciones y toma apuntes abajo para luego contestar las preguntas.

Apuntes

Dónde: . . . .

Con quién: . . . .

Cuándo: . . . .

El viaje: . . . .

Nombre de la estación de esquí: . . . . . .

Al llegar: . . . .

Por la noche: . . . .

Un día diferente: . . . .

¿Qué tal el viaje?: . . . .

Otros: . . . .

Vocabulario
El autocar = the coach
El bastón = the ski stick/pole
Sacarse el forfait = to buy a ski pass
De hecho = in fact
La pista de esquí = the ski slope
Había muchísima niebla = it was
very foggy

Exercise 6.19

¡Escribe!
Traduce este diario de Carlos al español.

Monday

I got up at 8 o'clock. I left the house at 9 and went to school by bus. At school I did nothing. I finished at 2 and went to Bar Niza. I saw Ana and we ate together. I ordered a ham sandwich and Ana ordered a salad. We spoke about the film we saw the other day and arranged to meet later to see a French film that they're showing at Multicines. I went home. I did my homework and then watched the television. I went to the cinema and waited and waited. She didn't arrive. I think she thinks I go out with too many girls.

Exercise 6.20

¡Escribe!
Now write a diary entry of your own for what you did on a day earlier this week. You should aim to write approximately 70 words. The vocabulary on the right may prove useful.

Vocabulario
Despertarse = to wake up
Levantarse = to get up
Ducharse = to have a shower
Desayunar = to have breakfast
Hacer los deberes = to do one's homework
Cenar = to have dinner
Acostarse = to go to bed

The imperfect tense

The imperfect tense is another tense that you will find vital to record events and descriptions in the past. Unlike the preterite tense, however, the imperfect is used for events and descriptions that are not finite, i.e. that have an element of continuity about them. If, for example, we wanted to say 'Carlos went to the cinema every Saturday', we are dealing with a situation which is **not** a one-off, but rather an event that happened on a regular basis. Equally, if we wanted to say 'he was eating' rather than 'he ate', the imperfect would also be required.

You will also learn in the future how the imperfect is required to describe people's characteristics in a past context. This would occur, for example, if we wanted to say 'Eva was tall and beautiful': *Eva **era** alta y muy guapa.* It helps if we remind ourselves that Eva was not tall and beautiful for a very fixed, limited period of time; these characteristics are lasting and continuous.

A further point to register at this point is that the imperfect is **always** used to describe **time** in the past. So, if we wanted to say 'it was 9 o'clock when he left', we would say ***eran** las nueve cuando salió.*

At this point, we will not be dealing with the imperfect in a particularly detailed fashion, but it certainly helps to have an understanding of the contexts in which it is used. It is, in fact, one of the easiest tenses to learn in that there are only 3 irregular verbs, one of which we have seen above (*ser*).

The imperfect tense of all –ar verbs

The imperfect tense of **all** *–ar* verbs is formed by removing the *–ar* ending and adding the following endings:

-aba	-ábamos
-abas	-abais
-aba	-aban

Study the following examples:

hablar			
Yo	hablaba	Nosotros	hablábamos
Tú	hablabas	Vosotros	hablabais
Él	hablaba	Ellos	hablaban

trabajar			
Yo	trabajaba	Nosotros	trabajábamos
Tú	trabajabas	Vosotros	trabajabais
Él	trabajaba	Ellos	trabajaban

The imperfect tense of all –er and –ir verbs except ser, ver, ir

The imperfect tense of all *–er* and *–ir* verbs except *ser, ver, ir* is formed by removing the *–er* or *–ir* ending and adding the following endings:

-ía	-íamos
-ías	-íais
-ía	-ían

Study the following examples:

hacer			
Yo	hacía	Nosotros	hacíamos
Tú	hacías	Vosotros	hacíais
Él	hacía	Ellos	hacían

decir			
Yo	decía	Nosotros	decíamos
Tú	decías	Vosotros	decíais
Él	decía	Ellos	decían

Exercise 6.21

¡Escribe!
Pon la palabra adecuada en cada hueco:

1. Yo ……..(hacer) mis deberes cuando sonó el teléfono.
2. Ellos …….. (hablar) con su abuela todos los domingos.
3. Nosotros … …….. (acostarse) tarde todas las noches.
4. …….. (hacer) mucho calor ese día.
5. Ella …….. (esquiar) cuando empezó a nevar.

> **Vocabulario**
> *Sonar* = to ring

Exercise 6.22

¡Escribe!
Traduce las frases de Exercise 6.21 al inglés.

Exercise 6.23

¡Escribe!
Each of the following five sentences has a gap for one use of the imperfect tense and one use of the preterite. As in Exercise 6.21 the verbs are provided in brackets. Write the correct form of each verb in the gaps provided:

1. Jorge …….. (comer) cuando …….. (entrar) Pedro.
2. Yo …….. (estar) en Italia cuando Inglaterra …….. (ganar) la copa.
3. Cuando Pepe …….. (salir) del cine …….. (llover).
4. María …….. (hablar) con su hermana cuando le …….. (picar) un mosquito.
5. Cuando nosotros …….. (ir) a la playa …….. (hacer) mucho sol y calor.

> **Vocabulario**
> *Picar* = to sting (insects)

Exercise 6.24

¡Escribe!
Traduce las frases de Exercise 6.23 al inglés.

Exercise 6.25

CD2: 33

¡Lee y escucha!
Lee o escucha a Pedro hablando de la corrida de toros que vio con Jorge, y apunta abajo todos los ejemplos del pretérito y del imperfecto. Luego, traduce la conversación al inglés.

> **Vocabulario**
> *El traje de luces* = the 'suit of lights' (bullfighter's costume)
> *La faena* = the bullfighter's display/performance

Vocabulario 6.1

And now for our final vocabulary, to carry you through until we meet again in Book 3.

Vocabulario 6.1

El actor = the actor

Además = besides

El ambiente = the atmosphere

Apetecer = to feel like

El autocar = the coach

El bastón = the ski-stick/pole

El grupo = the band/group

El sonido = the sound

El taller = the garage/mechanic's

El traje de luces = the bullfighter's costume

La entrada = the ticket

La faena = the bullfighter's display/performance

Habia muchísima niebla = it was very foggy

Has hecho = in fact

La llamada = the call

La pista de esquí = the ski-slope

Las procesiones = the Easter Week holy processions

La sala = the screen number (cinema)

Céntrico = central

Conseguir = to get

Darse cuenta de = to realise

Echar de menos = to miss (a person, place etc)

Emocionante = exciting

Estar hecho polvo = to be distraught/really tired (colloq.)

Había = there was/were

Invitar = to pay for someone else

Lleno = full

Lo de = the business about

Me da igual = it's all the same to me

Merecer la pena = to be worthwhile

Obsesionado = obsessed

Picar = to sting (insects)

Poner = to show (a film)

Quedar = to arrange to meet

Sacarse el forfait = to buy a ski-pass

Sentir = to be sorry about

Ser un punto = to be fantastic

La sesión = a showing/screening

A la sombra = in the shade

Sonar = to ring (telephone)

La taquilla = the box office

Tardar = to take time to do something

Tener enchufe = to have contacts

Summary of unit

At the end of this unit

You should now be able to: buy tickets for a range of different entertainments, offer alternatives and make arrangements; make plans with friends to go to an event; describe an outing in the past tense, including details about where you went, with whom, and how you got there. You may also be able to include extra details about times and descriptions of people and places.

Vocabulario: español-inglés

a = to, at
a causa de = because of
a diario = daily
a eso de = around (time)
a la sal = cooked in salt
a la una = at one o'clock
a las dos = at two o'clock
a lo mejor = probably
a mano... = on the....hand side
a menudo = often
a mi juicio = in my judgement
a veces = sometimes
a ver si = let's see whether, let's hope that
abdominal, el = sit-up
abogado, el = the lawyer
abrazo, el = hug, embrace; *un abrazo* = with best wishes
abrigo, el = coat, overcoat
abril (masc.) = April
abrir = to open
abuela, la = grandmother
abuelo, el = grandfather
aburrido = boring
academia, la = academy
aceite, el = oil
aceituna, la = olive
acento, el = accent
acompañar = to accompany
acordarse (ue) = to remember
acostarse (ue) = to go to bed
actividad, la = activity
activo = active
actor, el = actor
actuar = to perform
acuario = aquarius (star sign)
acuático = aquatic
acuerdo, el = agreement
acuesto: see *acostarse (ue)*
adecuado = adequate, appropriate
adelgazar = to lose weight
además = besides
adiós = goodbye
adivinar = to guess
adjetivo, el = adjective
¿adónde? = where to?
afeitarse = to shave

afición, la = pastime, hobby
aficionado, el = fan, supporter
afueras, las = outskirts
agencia de viajes, la = travel agents
agenda, la = diary, address book
agosto (masc.) = August
agradable = pleasant
agrario = agricultural
agregar = to add
agricultura, la = agriculture
agua, el (fem.) = water
aguantar = to put up with, stand, tolerate
ahora = now
ahora mismo = right now
aire acondicionado, el = air-conditioning
ajedrez, el = chess
ajo, el = garlic
al ajillo = cooked in garlic
al extranjero = abroad
al fin de = at the end of
al lado de = next to
albóndiga, la = meatball
alcanzar = to reach, go up to
alegre = happy
alemán = German
Alemania (fem.) = Germany
alfabeto, el = alphabet
alfombra, la = carpet
algo = something
algo, tomar = to have a drink
algodón, el = cotton
algún, alguna = some
algunas veces = sometimes
aliñar = to dress (salads)
aliño, el = dressing
allá = there (in the distance)
allí = there (quite near)
almacén, el = department store
almeja, la = clam
almorzar (ue) = to have lunch
almuerzo, el = lunch
alto = tall
alumno/a, el/la = pupil
ama (fem.) *de casa, el* = housewife
amarillo = yellow
ambiente, el = atmosphere

América (fem.) = America
americano = American
amiga, la = friend (fem.)
amigo, el = friend (masc.)
añadir = to add
¡anda! = come on, come off it!
andaluz = from the region of Andalucía
andando = on foot
animal, el = animal, pet
anorak, el = anorak
año que viene, el = next year
año, el = the year
antes de (+ infin.) = before -ing
antibióticos, los = antibiotics
antipático = horrible, unkind
antropología, la = anthropology
apartado postal (*apdo. postal*), *el* = p.o. box
aparte (adverb) = apart
apellidarse = to be called (surname)
apellido, el = surname
apetecer = to feel like
apodo, el = nickname
aprender = to learn
aprobar (ue) = to pass (an examination)
apunte, el = note
aquí = here
araña, la = spider
árbol, el = tree
Argentina (fem.) = Argentina
argentino = Argentinian
aries = aries (star sign)
armario, el = wardrobe, cupboard
arreglar = to fix
arreglarse = to get ready
arriba = above, upstairs
arroz con leche, el = rice-pudding
arroz, el = rice
arte, el = art
artículo, el = article
asado = roast/roasted
así = like that
así que = so, so then
asignatura, la = subject (school)
aspirina, la = aspirin
asqueroso = disgusting
atender = to serve
atletismo, el = athletics
atún, el = tuna
aula (fem.), *el* = classroom
Australia (fem.) = Australia
australiano = Australian

autobús, el = bus
autocar, el = coach
autovía, la = dual-carriageway
ayer = yesterday
ayudar = to help
ayuntamiento, el = town hall
azúcar, el = sugar
azúcar moreno, el = brown sugar
azul = blue
azul marino = navy blue
baca, la = roof-rack
bailar = to dance
bajar = to go down
bajo = short (height), low
baloncesto, el = basketball
balonmano, el = handball
bañador, el = swimming costume
bañarse = to have a bath, to swim in the sea
banco, el = bench
banco, el = bank
banda, la = band/group
bañera, la = bath
baño, el = bathroom
bar, el = bar
bar de tapas, el = tapas bar
barato = cheap
barbaridad, la = barbarism
barca, la = small boat
barco, el = boat
bastante = quite, enough
bastar = to be enough, sufficient
bastón, el = ski-stick
batido, el = milkshake
batir = to beat, mix, whisk
beber = to drink
bebida, la = drink
belén, el = nativity scene
belga = Belgian
Bélgica (fem.) = Belgium
besugo, el = sea bream
biblioteca, la = library
bici, la (abbreviation) = bike
bicicleta, la = bicycle
bien = well, good (when asking how someone is)
biología, la = biology
blanco = white
blusa, la = blouse
boca, la = mouth
bocadillo, el = sandwich
boli, el (abbreviation) = pen
bolígrafo, el = pen, biro

bollo, el = bun
bolso, el = bag, purse
bonito = pretty, nice-looking
boquerón, el = anchovy
bota, la = boot
botellín, el = little bottle
brazo, el = arm
brújula, la = compass
¡buen viaje! = have a good trip!
buenas noches = good night
buenas tardes = good afternoon
bueno (buen before masc. sing. noun) = good
buenos días = good morning, hello
bufanda, la = scarf
burro, el = donkey
buscar = to look for
butaca, la = armchair
caballo, el = horse
cabeza, la = head
cacao, el = cocoa
cada = each, every
cada vez más = more and more
cadera, la = hip
caer = to fall
café (con leche), el = (white) coffee
cafetería, la = café
cajetilla, la = packet
calamar, el = squid
calamares a la romana, los = squid cooked in batter
calcetín, el = sock
calculadora, la = calculator
calibre, el = calibre
caliente = hot
callarse = to be quiet
calle, la = street
calor, el = heat
calzar = to be of a certain shoe size
cama, la = bed
camarero/a, el/la = waiter, waitress
cambia de papel = swap around, change roles
cambiar = change
camino de = on the way to
camisa, la = shirt
camiseta, la = t-shirt
camiseta polo, la = short-sleeved sports shirt
campeón, el = champion
campeonato, el = championship
campo, el = countryside, field
caña de azúcar, la = sugar cane
Canadá (masc.) = Canada

Canarias, las = the Canaries
cancela, la = iron gate
cáncer = cancer (star sign)
cansado = tired
cantina, la = canteen, dining room
capilla, la = chapel
capital, la = the capital (city)
capricornio = capricorn (star sign)
cara, la = face
Caribe el (masc.) = Caribbean
caries, la = plaque
cariño = darling
cariñoso = loving, affectionate
carne, la = meat, flesh
carné de indentidad, el = I.D. card
carpeta, la = file, folder
carretera, la = road
carta, la = letter, playing card
casa, la = house
casado = married
casi = almost
castaño = chestnut-coloured
castellano = castilian, spanish
castillo, el = castle
catalán = Catalan
catedral, la = cathedral
catorce = fourteen
cava, el = champagne
cebolla, la = onion
ceja, la = eye-brow
celebrar = to celebrate
cena, la = dinner
cenar = to have one's evening meal
céntrico = in the centre
centro, el = centre
centroamérica (fem.) = central America
cerca (de) = close, near (to)
cercano = near (adj.)
cerdo, el = pork
cereales, los = cereals
cerradura, la = lock
cerveza, la = beer
chabola, la = shack
chalet, el = a detached villa
champiñón, el = mushroom
chanclas, las = flip-flops
chándal, el = tracksuit
chapuza, la = odd job
chaqueta, la = jacket
charlar = to chat
chica, la = girl

chico, el = boy
chiflar = to be crazy about (works like *gustar*)
Chile (masc.) = Chile
chileno = Chilean
China (fem.) = China
chino = Chinese
chocolate, el = chocolate
chorizo, el = red spicy sausage
chorrito, un = a few drops of
chubascos, los = showers
chuches, las (chucherías) = sweets
chuleta, la = chop
chulo = cool (colloquial)
chupar = to suck
ciclismo, el = cycling
cielo, el = sky, heaven
cien(to) = hundred
ciencias, las = the sciences; science
cigarillo, el = cigarette
cinco = five
cincuenta = fifty
cine, el = cinema
cinta, la = the tape
cinturón, el = belt
ciudad, la = the city
clara, la = shandy
claro = of course, clear, bright
claros, los = clear patches
clase, la = class, classroom
clásico = classical
clima, el = climate
club, el = club
coca cola, la = coke
cocer (ue) = to cook
coche, el = car
cochinillo, el = suckling pig
cocido, el = stew
cocina, la = kitchen
cocinar = to cook
cocinero, el = cook
coco, el = coconut
codo, el = elbow
coger = to take, catch
colacao, el = a popular chocolate drink
cole, el = school (shortened form)
colegio, el = school (primary)
coliflor, la = cauliflower
colocar = to put, place
Colombia (fem.) = Colombia
colombiano = Colombian
color, el = colour

columna, la = column
comedor, el = dining room
comentario, el = commentary
comenzar (ie) = to begin
comer = to eat
comida grasa, la = fatty foods
comida, la = food, meal, lunch
como = as, like
¿cómo? = how?
como consecuencia = as a result
¿cómo es? = what is....like?
¿cómo se llama usted? = what is your name? (formal)
¿cómo son? = what are....like?
¿cómo te llamas? = what is your name? (informal)
cómodo = comfortable
compact disc, el = cd, cd player
compañero/a, el/la = companion
comparar = to compare
completar = to complete
completo = complete
compra, la = shopping
comprar = to buy
comprender = to understand
con = with
con gas = fizzy
concierto, el = concert
conejo, el = rabbit
congelador, el = freezer
conocer = to know (a person or place)
conseguir = to get
consejo, el = advice
conserje, el = caretaker
consistir en = to consist of
construir = to build
contar = to tell, count
contento = content, happy
contestar = to answer
contigo = with you
continuo = continuous
convencer = to convince
conversación, la = conversation
copa, la = glass, drink with mixer
corbata, la = cravat, neck-tie
cordero, el = lamb
corona, la = crown
correcto = correct
corregir (i) = to correct
correo electrónico, el = e-mail
correos = post office

correr = to run
correspondiente = corresponding
corresponsal, el = correspondent, (pen-pal)
corrida, la = bullfight
corrida de toros, la = bullfight
cortar = to cut
cortar en juliana = to cut into thin slices
corto = short (length)
cosa, la = thing
costa, la = coast
Costa Rica (fem.) = Costa Rica
costumbre, la = habit
creer = to think, believe
cruzar = to cross
cuaderno, el = exercise book
cuadrilla, la = team
cuadro, el = painting
¿cuál? = which? what? (interrog.)
cualquier cosa = anything
cuándo = when
¿cuándo? = when (interrog.)
cuando vengas = when you come
¿cuánto/a/os/as? = how much, many
cuarenta = forty
cuarto = fourth
cuarto, el = room; quarter
cuarto de baño, el = bathroom
cuatro = four
cuatrocientos = four hundred
cubano = Cuban
cucharadita, una = a teaspoonful
cuece: see *cocer (ue)*
cuello, el = neck
cuéntame = tell me
cuerpo, el = body
cuero, el = leather
cuidado, el = care
culebrón, el = soap opera
cultivo, el = crop
cumpleaños, el = the birthday
cumplir = to reach the age of
curiosidad, la = curiosity
curso, el = (school) year
danés = Danish
dar = to give
darse cuenta de = to realise
de = of, from
de acuerdo ¡de acuerdo! = agreed!
de camino = on the way
de hecho = in fact
de lujo = luxury, high class

de media = on average
de moda = fashionable, trendy
de momento = for the time being
de nada = not at all, it's my pleasure
de primer plato = as a first course
de segundo = as a second course
de todas formas = at any rate, anyhow, anyway
de vez en cuando = from time to time
debajo de = under
deber = to ought (must)
deberes, los = homework
debería = I/he/she ought
deberías = you should
decidir = to decide
décimo = tenth
decir (i) (1st person singular: *digo*) = to say
dedo, el = finger
dejar = to leave, allow, drop off
dejar cocer a fuego suave = to let simmer
del: de + el = of the
delante de = in front of
deletrear = to spell out
delgado = thin, slim
demasiado = too/too much
dentro de x minutos = in x minutes' time
dependienta, la = shop assistant
deporte, el = sport
deportes, los = sports, games
deportes acuáticos, los = water sports
deportista = sporty
deportivo = sporty
derecho = right
desarrollar = to develop
desayunar = to have breakfast
descansar = to rest
describir = to describe
descripción, la = description
descubrir = to discover
descuento, el = discount
desde = from
desde luego = of course
despacio = slow
despejado = clear
despertarse (ie) = to wake up
después = afterwards
después de = after
detalle, el = detail
detrás de = behind
dí (from decir) = say
día, el = the day
diagnóstico, el = diagnosis

diálogo, el = dialogue
diario = daily
dibujar = to draw
dibujo, el = art, picture, drawing
diccionario, el = dictionary
dice: see *decir*
dicho esto = that said
diciembre (masc.) = december
diecinueve = nineteen
dieciocho = eighteen
dieciséis = sixteen
diecisiete = seventeen
diente, el = tooth
dieta, la = diet
diez = ten
diferente = different
dígame = hello
Dinamarca (fem.) = Denmark
dinero, el = the money
dirección, la = address
director, el = headteacher (male)
directora, la = headteacher (female)
disciplinado = disciplined
discoteca, la = disco
discurso, el = speech
disfrutar = to enjoy
divertido = fun, funny, amusing
diversiones, las = pastimes
dividido = divided
dividir = to divide
doblar = to turn
doce = twelve
doler = to hurt
dolor, el = pain, ache
domicilio, el = residence
domingo = Sunday
dominó, el = dominoes
donde = where
dónde ¿dónde? = where?
¿dónde demonios has estado? = where on earth
    have you been?
donut, el = donut
dorado = golden, gold-coloured
dormilón, el = someone who sleeps a lot
dormir (*ue*) = to sleep
dormitorio, el = bedroom
dos = two
doscientos = two hundred
drogas, las = drugs
ducha, la = shower
ducharse = to have a shower

dueño, el = owner
dulce = sweet
durante = during
durar = to last
e = and
echar = to add, post
echar de menos = to miss (a person/place)
economía, la = economy
Ecuador (masc.) = Ecuador
edad, la = age
edificio, el = building
Edimburgo (masc.) = Edinburgh
educación física, la = p.e. (physical education)
educación secundaria obligatoria, la = compulsory
    secondary education (i.e. secondary school)
educado = polite, cultured
egoísta = selfish
egoísta, el = the selfish person
ejemplo, el = example
ejercicio, el = exercise
ejército, el = the army
el = the (masculine singular)
él = he
el que = (that) which
El Salvador (masc.) = El Salvador
elaboración, la = preparation
elegir = to choose
ella = she
ellos/as = they
embutidos, los = products such as chorizo,
    salchichón, jamón
emilio, el (slang) = e-mail
emocionante = exciting
emparejar = to match up
empastar = to fill
empezar (*ie*) = to start, begin
empujar = to push
en = in, on
en coche = by car
en cuanto = as soon as
en cuanto a = as regards
en efectivo = by cash
en general = generally
en lugar de = instead of
en mi opinión = in my opinion
en punto = on the dot, o'clock
en seguida = at once
en total = in total
en vez de = instead of
encantado (de conocerte) = pleased (to meet you)
encantar = to love (works like *gustar*)

encerrar = to shut, lock up
encontrar (ue) = to meet, to find
encontrarse bien/mal = to feel good/bad
encuesta, la = survey
enero (masc.) = January
enfadado = angry
enfrente (de) = opposite (to)
engordar = to put on weight
enjuague, el = mouthwash
ensalada, la = salad
ensaladera, la = salad bowl
enseñar = to show, teach
entenderse = to get on with
entonces = then, so then
entrada, la = ticket
entrar = to enter, go in
entre = between
entretenido = entertaining
entrevista, la = interview
entrevistar = to interview
época, la = period, time
equilibrado = balanced
equipo, el = team, equipment
equitación, la = (horse) riding
era (imperfect tense of *ser*) = he/she/it was
eres (from *ser*) = you (sing.) are
es (from *ser*) = he/she/it is
es decir = that is to say, i.e.
escalfar = to boil (an egg), to poach
escaparse = to escape, get away
escarcha, la = frost
escocés = Scottish
Escocia (fem.) = Scotland
escolar (adj.) = (of a) school
escorpio = scorpion (star sign)
escribir = to write
escuchar = to listen
escuela, la = school
escurrir = to drain, strain
ese, esa, esos, esas = that, those (demonstrative adjective)
ése, ésa, ésos, ésas = that, those (demonstrative pronoun)
esfuerzo, el = effort
eso = compulsory secondary education
eso es = that's right
espada, la = sword
espaguetis, los = spaghetti
espalda, la = back
España (fem.) = Spain
español = Spanish

español, el = Spanish (language)
especial = special, fussy
especialmente = especially
espectáculo, el = spectacle
espejo, el = mirror
espinacas, las = spinach
esquí, el = skiing
esquí aquático, el = water-skiing
esquiar = to ski
esquina, la = corner (street/ road)
estaba = it was
estación, la = station, season
estación de esquí, la = ski resort
estadio, el = stadium
Estados Unidos, los = USA
estancia, la = the stay
estantería, la = bookcase
estar = to be
estar a punto de = to be on the point of
estar asado = to be boiling hot
estar bueno = to be tasty
estar de rebajas = to be on sale
estar despejado = to be clear
estar harto = to be fed up
estar hecho polvo = to be distraught/extremely tired
estar loco por = to be crazy about
estar nublado = to be cloudy
estar seguro = to be sure
estarán = they will be
este, el = east
éste/a/o = this (one)
estereotipo, el = stereotype
esto = this (thing)
estropeado = broken (down)
estuche, el = pencil-case
estudiante, el/la = student
estudiar = to study
estupendo = superb/great
ética, la = ethics, PSHE
euro, el = euro
evitar = to avoid
exactamente = exactly
examen, el = exam
excepto = except (for)
exótico = exotic
expedido (esped.) = issued
explicar = to explain
explosivo, el = explosive
extrañar = to surprise
extranjero = foreign, abroad

extranjero, el = foreigner
extremo meridional, el = the southern end
extrovertido = outgoing, extrovert
fácil = easy
fácilmente = easily
faena, la = bullfighter's display/performance
falda, la = skirt
falla, la = ornate cardboard figure
falso = false
familia, la = family
famoso = famous
fanta = fanta (popular brand name for fizzy drinks)
fantástico = fantastic
farmacéutico, el = chemist, pharmacist
farmacia, la = chemists
fastidio, el = nuisance, boredom
fatal = awful
favorito = favourite
febrero (masc.) = February
fecha, la = date
feliz = happy, good-natured
fenomenal = brilliant
feo = ugly
feria, la = fair, market, show
ficha, la = form, record-card
fideo, el = noodle
fiesta, la = the party, festival
fijarse en = to take notice of
filete, el = fillet
fin, el = end
fin de semana, el = weekend
final de, el = the end of
finlandés = Finnish
Finlandia (fem.) = Finland
física, la = physics
físico, el = appearance
flan, el = the crème caramel
flan con nata, el = crème caramel with cream
flor, la = flower
florido = flowery
folleto, el = brochure
footing, el = hiking
forfait, el = ski-pass
forma, la = shape, form
francés = French
francés, el = French (language)
Francia (fem.) = France
frase, la = sentence
frecuencia, con poca = rarely
frecuencia, la = frequency

fregadero, el = sink
fregar (ie) = to scrub (wash dishes)
fresco = fresh, cool
fresquito = cool, fresh
frío, hacer = to be cold
fruta, la = fruit
fue (from *ser*) = he/she/it was
fuera = outside
fuerte = strong
fumar = to smoke
funcionar = to work
furioso = angry, furious
fútbol, el = football
fútbol sala, el = indoor (5-a-side) football
gafas, las = glasses
gafas de sol, las = sunglasses
galaxia, la = galaxy
galés = Welsh
Gales (masc.) = Wales
galleta, la = biscuit
gamba, la = prawn
gana, la = wish, desire
ganga, la = bargain
garbanzo, el = chickpea
gas, el = gas
gastar = to spend (money)
gato, el = cat
gemela, la = twin
géminis = gemini
general = general
generoso = generous
genial = great
gente, la (used in singular) = people
geografía, la = geography
gibraltareño = from Gibraltar
gimnasia, la = gymnastics
golf, el = golf
golfo, el = the gulf
goma, la = rubber
gordo = fat
gorra, la = cap, beret
gracias = thank you, thanks
gracioso = funny
grado, el = degree
gramo, un = a gram
grande = big
grandes almacenes, los = department store
granja, la = farm
Grecia (fem.) = Greece
griego = Greek
gris = grey

gritar = to yell
grupo, el = group, band
guante, el = glove
guapo = handsome, pretty
guarnición, la = garnish
Guatemala (fem.) = Guatemala
guay = super, great, cool (informal)
guitarra, la = guitar
gustar = to please, like
gusto, el = taste, pleasure, liking for
ha habido = there has been
ha invitado = he/she has invited
había = there was/were
hábil = skilful
habitación, la = room
habitante, el/la = inhabitant
hablar = to speak
hablar por teléfono = to speak on the telephone
hace buen tiempo, hace bueno = it's fine weather
hace (mucho) calor = it's (very) hot
hace fresco = it's cool, chilly
hace (mucho) frío = it's (very) cold
hace mal tiempo, hace malo = it's bad weather
hace sol = it's sunny
hace viento = it's windy
hace x grados = it's x degrees
hacer (irreg.) = to do, make
hacer ejercicio = to do exercise
hacer falta = to be necessary
hacer footing = to go jogging
hacer la compra = to do the shopping
hacer los deberes = to do one's homework
hacer vela = to go sailing
hacerse (irreg.) = to become
hamaca, la = hammock
hambre (fem.), *el* = hunger
hamburguesa, la = hamburger
hámster, el = hamster
harto, estar = to be fed up
¿has decidido? = have you decided?
has dormido = you have slept
has hecho = you have done
hasta = until, even
hasta la vista = see you later
hasta luego = see you later
hay = there is, there are
hay escarcha = it's frosty
hay hielo = it's icy
hay niebla = it's foggy
hay que = one has to
hay tormenta = it's stormy

he dicho = I have said
he ido = I've gone
he viajado = I have travelled
helado = frozen
helado, el = ice-cream
helicóptero, el = helicopter
hemos esquiado = we have skied
hemos tenido que = we have had to
hermana, la = sister
hermanastra, la = step-sister
hermanastro, el = step-brother
hermano, el = brother
hervir = to boil
hielo, el = ice
hierba, la = grass
hierro, el = iron
higiene bucal, la = oral hygiene
hija, la = daughter
hija única, la = only child (female)
hijo, el = son
hijo único, el = only child (male)
hilo dental, el = dental floss
hispano = Hispanic, Spanish
historia, la = history, story
hizo (from *hacer*) = (he/she) did
hola = hi, hello
Holanda (fem.) = Holland
holandés = Dutch
hombre, el = man
hombro, el = shoulder
Honduras (fem.) = Honduras
hora, la = hour, time
horario, el = timetable
horno, el = oven
horóscopo, el = horoscope
horrible = horrible
hortalizas, las = vegetables
hortera = tacky
hospital, el = hospital
hotel, el = hotel
hoy = today
hoy en día = nowadays
hueco, el = blank, gap
huevo, el = egg
huevo relleno, el = egg with stuffing
¡id! (from *ir*) = go!
idioma, el = language
ídolo, el = idol
iglesia, la = church
igual = the same, equal
igual que = same as

igualmente = likewise
ilustrado = illustrated
imagen, la = image, picture
imbécil = stupid
imperativo, el = imperative
importante = important
impresión, la = impression
incluso = even
incorporar = to add
increíble = incredible
indicar = to indicate, point out
indio = indian
infinitivo, el = infinitive
inflamado = inflamed
inflarse de comer = to stuff oneself
información, la = information
informática, la = ICT
Inglaterra (fem.) = England
inglés = English
inglés, el = English (the language)
ingrediente, el = ingredient
inhumano = inhuman
injusto = unjust
instituto, el = school (secondary)
instrucción, la = instruction
inteligente = intelligent
intentar = to try (attempt)
intercambio, el = the exchange
interesante = interesting
interesar = to interest
inventar = to invent
investigar = to research, find out
invierno, el = winter
invitar = to pay for someone else
ir (irreg) = to go
ir a (+ infin.) = to be going to do (simple future)
ir de tiendas, ir de compras = to go shopping
Irlanda (fem.) = Ireland
irlandés = Irish
isla, la = isle, island
Italia (fem.) = Italy
italiano = Italian
izquierda = left
jabón, el = soap
jamón, el = ham
Japón (masc.) = Japan
japonés = Japanese
jardín, el = garden
jarra, la = jar
joven = young
judía verde, la = green bean

juego, el = game
jueves = thursday
jugar = to play
julio (masc.) = July
junio (masc.) = June
juntos = together
justo = just, right
kilómetro, el = kilometre
kiwi, el = kiwi
la = the (fem. sing.)
laboral = working (adj.)
laboratorio, el = laboratory
lado, el = side
ladrón, el = thief
lámpara, la = lamp
lápiz, el = pencil
largo = long
lasaña, la = the lasagne
latín, el = Latin
lavabo, el = basin
lavadora, la = washing-machine
lavaplatos, el = dishwasher
lavar = to wash
lavarse = to wash oneself, to get washed
le = him, to him, to her
leche, la = milk
lechuga, la = lettuce
lectura, la = reading
leer = to read
lejos (de) = far (from)
lengua, la = language
lenguado, el = sole (fish)
lento = slow
leo = leo (star sign)
león, el = lion
les = to them
levantarse = to get up
libra = libra (star sign)
libre = free
libro, el = book
lidiar = to bullfight
ligero = light (adj.)
limitar con = to border with
limón, el = lemon
limpiarse los dientes = to brush one's teeth
liso = straight (hair)
literatura, la = literature
llamada, la = call
llamarse = to be called
llegada, la = arrival
llegar = to arrive

lleno = full
llevar = to carry, wear
llevarse = to take (buy)
llevarse = to get on with
llevarse bien/fatal con = to get on well/badly with
llover (ue) = to rain
llueve = it rains
lluvioso = rainy
lo = it (direct object pronoun)
lo bueno = the good thing
lo de = the business about
lo malo = the bad thing
lo mismo = the same thing
lo pasé bomba = I had a fantastic time
lo peor = the worst thing
lo que quieras = whatever you want
lo siento = I'm sorry
localidad, la = location, town
loco = crazy
Londres (masc.) = London
los = the (masc. pl.); them (direct object pronoun)
¿los habéis hecho? = have you done them?
lubina, la = sea bass
luego = then, later
lunes = monday
luz, la (pl. luces) = light
madrastra, la = step-mother
madre, la = mother
madrileño = from Madrid
madrugada, la = dawn, early morning
magnífico = great, superb
malagueño = from Málaga
malo (mal before masc. sing. noun) = bad
mamá = mum, mummy
mañana = tomorrow
mañana, la = the morning
mandar = to order, send
mandarina, la = mandarine
mano, la = hand
mantecado, el = ice cream, lardy cake
mantenerse en forma = to keep fit
mantenimiento, el = maintenance, up keep
mantis religiosa, la = praying mantis
manzana, la = apple
mapa, el = map
mar, el = sea
marca, la = brand
marchoso = extrovert
marido, el = husband
marisco, el = shellfish
marrón = brown

martes = Tuesday
mártir, el/la = martyr
martirizar = to torture, martyr
marzo (masc.) = March
más = more, most, plus (+)
mascota, la = pet
matador, el = the bullfighter who kills the bull
matar = to kill
matemáticas, las = maths
máximo = top, highest
mayo (masc.) = may
mayonesa, la = mayonnaise
mayor = older, oldest, bigger, biggest
mazapán, el = marzipan
me = me, to me, myself
me chifla = I love, I'm mad about
me da igual = it's all the same to me
me gustaría = I would like (conditional tense)
me gustó = I liked
medias, las = tights, stockings
medicamento, el = medicine
médico, el = doctor
medio = half
medio hecho = medium (cooked)
medir (i) = to be of a certain height
mejicano : see *mexicano*
Méjico (masc.) : see *México*
mejillón, el = mussel
mejor = better, best
mejorar = to improve, get better
melón, el = melon
mencionar = to mention
menor = younger, smaller
menos = less, minus (-), except
menos cuarto = quarter to
¡menos mal! = thank goodness!
mentir (ie) = to tell a lie
mentira, la = lie
mercado, el = market
merecer la pena = to be worthwhile
merendar (ie) = to have a snack, to have tea
meridional = southern
merienda, la = afternoon snack
merluza, la = hake (fish)
mes, el = month
mesa, la = table
mesita de noche, la = bedside table
meter = to put
metro, el = metre; the underground (train system)
México (masc.) = Mexico
mexicano = Mexican

mezclar = to mix
mi(s) = my
miedo, el = fear
mientras que = while
miércoles = Wednesday
mil = thousand
millón, el = million
mimo, el = mime
mina, la = mine
mineral = mineral
minería, la = mining
minero = mining (adj.)
minifalda, la = miniskirt
minuto, el = minute
mirar = to look at, watch
misa, la = mass
mismo = same
mixto = mixed (adj.)
mochila, la = rucksack, school-bag
moderno = modern
momento, el = moment
moneda, la = currency
montaña, la = mountain
montar a caballo = to go riding
montar en bici(cleta) = to ride a bike
montón de, un = loads of, piles of
morado = purple
moreno = dark (colour)
mostaza, la = mustard
motociclismo, el = motorcycling
móvil, el = mobile telephone
muchas gracias = thank you very much
muchísimo = very much
mucho = much, many, a lot
muebles, los = furniture
muela, la = molar
mujer, la = woman, wife
muleta, la = cape
multiplicado = multiplied
multiplicar = to multiply
mundial = of the world (adj)
mundo, el = world
municipal = municipal
músculo, el = muscle
museo, el = museum
música, la = music
muy = very
muy buenas = hi there
nacer = to be born
nacimiento, el = birth
nació = (he/she) was born

nacionalidad, la = nationality
nada = nothing
nadador, el = swimmer
nadar = to swim
naranja = orange (the colour)
naranja, la = orange (the fruit)
nariz, la = nose
nata, la = cream
natación, la = swimming
natural = natural
navegante, el = sailor
navegar = to sail; to surf (e.g. the internet)
navidad, la = christmas
necesario = necessary
negro = black
nervioso = nervous, anxious
nevar (ie) = to snow
nevera, la = fridge
ni...ni = neither...nor
¡ni hablar! = no way!
Nicaragua (fem.) = Nicaragua
niebla, la = fog
nieta, la = grand-daughter
nieto, el = grandson
nieva: see *nevar (ie)*
nieve, la = snow
niña, la = girl, child (female)
ninguna parte = nowhere
ninguno (*ningún* before masc. sing. noun) = no, not any
niño, el = boy, child (male)
no = not, no
¡no fastidies! = you must be joking!
no había = there wasn't/weren't any
no importa = it doesn't matter
no seas tonta = don't be silly
noche, la = night
nochebuena, la = christmas eve
nochevieja, la = new year's eve
nocilla, la = a type of chocolate spread
nombre, el = the name
normal = normal, natural
normalmente = normally
norte, el = north
Noruega (fem.) = Norway
noruego = Norwegian
nos = us, to us, ourselves
nos hemos comido = we've eaten
nosotros/as = we
novecientos = nine hundred
noveno = ninth

noventa = ninety
novia, la = girlfriend
noviembre (masc.) = November
novio, el = boyfriend
nublado = cloudy
nuestro = our
nueve = nine
nuevo = new
número, el = the number
numeroso = numerous
nunca = never
o = or
o sea = i.e./ that's to say
obedecer = to obey
obligatorio = compulsory
obsesionado = obsessed
obsesionarse (con) = to become obsessive (about)
océano, el = ocean
ochenta = eighty
ocho = eight
ochocientos = eight hundred
octavo = eighth
octubre (masc.) = October
oeste, el = west
oficial = official
oficina de turismo, la = tourist information office
oficina, la = office
oiga = excuse me
ojo, el = eye
olvidar = to forget
once = eleven
opinar que = to think that
optativo = optional
orar = to pray
orden, el = order
ordenador, el = computer
orégano, el = oregano
oreja, la = ear
origen, el = origin
oro, el = gold (the metal)
os = you, to you, yourselves
otoño, el = autumn
otra vez = again, another time
otro = other
Pacífico, el = Pacific
padrastro, el = step-father
padre, el = father; parent
paella, la = paella
pagano = pagan
página, la = page
país, el = country

paisaje, el = countryside, landscape
pájaro, el = bird
palabra, la = word
pan, el = bread
panadería, la = bakery
panadero, el = the baker
Panamá (masc.) = Panama
pantalón, el = pair of trousers
papá = dad, daddy
papel, el = paper; piece of paper
para = for
para (+ infin.) = in order to
para chuparse los dedos = delicious (lit. to suck one's fingers)
paraguas, el = umbrella
Paraguay (masc.) = Paraguay
parecer = to appear, seem; *me parece que* = I think that
parecido = similar
pared, la = wall (of a building)
pareja, la = pair, partner
parque, el = park
párrafo, el = paragraph
parrilla, la = grill
partido, el = match, game, team
pasa, la = prune
pasado mañana = the day after tomorrow
pasar lista = to take the register
pasar por agua = to run under water
pasarlo bien = to have a good time
pasarlo bomba = to have a great time
pasatiempos, los = hobbies
pasta, la = pasta; cash (slang)
pastilla, la = pill
pastor alemán, el = German shepherd
patata, la = potato
patatas fritas, las = chips
patinaje, el = skating
patinar = to skate
patio, el = the courtyard, playground
patriótico = patriotic
patrona, la = patron
pavo, el = turkey
peatón, el = pedestrian
pechuga, la = breast (of chicken)
pedir (i) = to ask for
pegar con = to suit, go with
peinarse = to comb one's hair
pelar = to peel
película, la = film
pelirrojo = redhead, ginger

pelo, el = hair
pena, la = sorrow, trouble, pain
pendiente, el = earring
península, la = the peninsula (e.g. Spain & Portugal)
pensar (ie) = to think
pepino, el = cucumber
pequeño = small
pera, la = pear
perder (ie) = to lose
perdone = excuse me
perezoso = lazy
perfecto = perfect
periódico, el = newspaper
perjudicar = to harm, damage
permitir = to allow
pero = but
perro, el = dog
persona, la = person
personaje, el = celebrity, important person, character
Perú (masc.) = Peru
pesado = annoying
pesar = to weigh
pescado, el = fish
peso, el = weight; peso (unit of currency in some S. American countries)
petróleo, el = oil, petroleum
pez, el (plural peces) = fish
picar = to sting
pico, y = and a bit
pie, el = foot
piel, la = skin
pienso: see *pensar (ie)*
pierna, la = leg
pimiento, el = pepper
piña, la = pineapple
pintado = painted
pintor, el = painter
pirámide, la = pyramid
piscina, la = swimming pool
piscis = pisces (star sign)
piso, el = floor, flat
pista de esquí, la = ski-slope
pizarra, la = blackboard, whiteboard
pizca, una = a pinch (e.g. of salt)
pizza, la = pizza
planchado = ironed
planeta, el = planet
plano, el = plan
planta, la = floor (of apartment building)

plata, la = silver (the metal)
plátano, el = banana
plateado = silver (the colour)
plato, el = dish, course
playa, la = beach
plaza, la = square (of a town)
plaza de toros, la = bullring
poblado = bushy
pobre = poor
poco = a little (amount)
poco hecho = rare (cooked)
poder (ue) = to be able
policía, el = policeman
polideportivo, el = sports centre, sports hall
pollo, el = chicken
poner = to put/show a film
poner un disco = to play a record
ponerse = to put on, wear, become
ponerse a régimen = to go on a diet
ponerse en forma = to get fit
pop = pop (short for popular)
popular = popular
por = by, for, along, through; (+ infin.) in order to
por ciento = per cent
¿por dónde se va a? = how do I get to?
por ejemplo = for example
por eso = that's why
por este motivo = for this reason
por favor = please
por lo tanto = therefore, consequently
por primera vez = for the first time
¿por qué? = why?
por regla general = as a general rule
por supuesto = of course, naturally
porque = because
Portugal (masc.) = Portugal
portugués = Portugese
poseer = to have, possess
posición, la = position
póster, el = poster
postre, el = dessert, pudding
practicar = to practise, do, play (e.g. a sport)
precipitaciones, las = rain
preferido = favourite
preferir (ie) = to prefer
pregunta, la = question
preguntar = to ask (a question)
preocuparse (por) = to worry (about)
preparar = to prepare
prepararse = to prepare oneself, get ready
presentar = to present

presente = present (adj.)
presente, el = present (tense)
prestar = to lend
prima, la = cousin (female)
primario = primary
primavera, la = spring (the season)
primer plato, el = first course (of meal)
primero (*primer* before masc. sing. noun) = first
primo, el = cousin (male)
principal = main
privado = private
probar (ue) = to try, sample
probarse (ue) = to try on
problema, el = problem
procesiones, las = easter week holy processions
procurar = to try
producir = to produce
productor, el = producer
profesor, el = teacher (male)
profesora, la = teacher (female)
programa, el = programme
pronombre, el = pronoun
pronóstico del tiempo, el = weather forecast
pronto = quickly, promptly
pronunciar = to pronounce
provincia, la = province
próximo = next
proyector, el = projector
pueblecito, el = small town
pueblo, el = town, village
puede: see *poder (ue)*
puerta, la = door
pues = well, um, then
puesto que = since, because
punto débil, el = the weak spot
pupitre, el = desk
que = that (after a verb)
¿qué? = what?
¡que aproveche! = *bon apetit*, enjoy your meal!
¡qué asco! = how disgusting!
¡qué barbaridad! = how extraordinary!
¡qué gusto! = how nice!
¿qué hay? = how's it going?
¡qué ilusión! = how exciting!
¡qué lástima! = what a shame, pity
¡qué miedo! = how scary
¡qué pena! = what a shame, pity
¡qué pesado! = what a pain
¡qué raro! = how strange!
¡qué rico! = how delicious!
¡qué rollo! = what a pain/bore!

¡qué suerte! = how lucky
¿qué tal? = how are you?
¡que te mejores! = I hope you get better
¿qué te parece? = what do you think about it?
¡qué va! = no way!
que viene = that is coming, next
quedar = to arrange to meet
quedar = to be left, remain
quedarse = to take, keep (clothes), to stay
quedarse en casa = to stay at home
querer (ie) = to want
querer es poder = "where there's a will, there's a way"
querido = dear
queso, el = cheese
quien = who (relative pronoun)
¿quién? = who?
quiero: see *querer (ie)*
química, la = chemistry
quince = fifteen
quinientos = five hundred
quinto = fifth
quisiera = I would like
quitar = to take off, remove, switch off
quitarse la ropa = to get undressed
quizá(s) = perhaps, maybe
radio, la = radio
rápido = quick, quickly
raro = strange, odd
rato, el = (short) time
ratón, el = mouse
rayo, el = lightning
razón, la = reason
real = real, royal
Real Madrid, el = Real Madrid (football team)
rebaja, la = sale, reduction
receta, la = recipe
recibí = I received
recibir = to receive
recipiente, el = container
recoger = to meet, pick up
reconocer = to admit, recognise
recreo, el = break
recto = straight
redondo = round
reflexivo = reflexive
refrescarse = to cool down
refresco, el = soft drink
regalar = to give (as a present)
regalo, el = present
regañar = to tell off

región, la = region
regla, la = ruler, rule
regresar = to return
regular = okay; so, so; not bad
rehogar = to sauté
reina, la = queen
relajado = relaxed
relajarse = to 'chill out', relax
religión, la = religious studies, R.E.
rellenar = to fill in
reloj, el = watch, clock
remover = to stir
Renfe = spain's national railway network
repaso, el = revision
representado = represented
responsable = responsible
respuesta, la = the answer
restaurante, el = restaurant
resulta = the fact is/it transpires that
revista, la = magazine
rey, el = king
rezar = to pray
rico = tasty, rich
riquísimo = delicious
rizado = curly
rodaja, la = slice
rodilla, la = knee
rojo = red
rollo, el = bore, pain
ron, el = rum
ropa, la = clothes
rosa = pink
rosado = rosé (wine)
rotulador, el = marker pen
rubio = blonde, fair-skinned
rudo = rough
rugby, el = rugby
ruidoso = noisy
Rusia (fem.) = Russia
ruso = Russian
rutina, la = routine
sábado = saturday
saber = to know
sabor, el = taste
sabroso = tasty
sacapuntas, el = pencil sharpener
sacar = to take out, take (photos)
sacarse el forfait = to buy a ski-pass
sacarse el carné = to get ones driving licence
sagitario = sagittarius (star sign)
sal, la = salt

sala, la = room; screen number (cinema)
sala de estar, la = living room
sala de profesores, la = staff room
salchichón, el = spicy salami sausage
salir (1st pers. sing.: *salgo*) = to go out
salir con = to go out with
salir de tapas = to go out for tapas
salmón, el = salmon
salón, el = living room
salud, la = health
saludos = best wishes, greetings
sandalia, la = sandal
sano = healthy
santo, el = saint
se = one, himself/herself/themselves
se ha bebido = he has drunk
se habla = is spoken
se me da(n) bien = I'm good at
se me da(n) fatal = I'm bad at
se(p)tiembre (masc.) = September
seco = dry
secretaria, la = secretary
sector, el = sector
seguida, en = in a moment, right away
seguir (i)(1st person sing.: *sigo*) = to follow, continue
según = according to
segundo = second
segundo plato, el = main course (of meal)
seguro = sure, certain
seis = six
seiscientos = six hundred
semáforo, el = traffic-light
semana, la = week
Semana Santa, la = Holy Week (Easter)
señor = Mr, sir
señora = Mrs, madam
señores x, los = Mr and Mrs *x*
señorita = miss
sentar = to suit
sentar bien = to fit, suit
sentarse (ie) = to sit down
sentido, el = sense
sentido, tener = to make sense
sentir = to be sorry about, to feel
sentirse = to feel
septiembre (masc.) = September
séptimo = seventh
ser = to be
ser fuerte en = to be good at
ser un éxito = to be a success

ser un punto = to be fantastic (slang)
sería = it would be
sesenta = sixty
sesión, la = showing/screening
setecientos = seven hundred
setenta = seventy
sexto = sixth
si = if
sí = yes
sidra, la = cider
siempre = always
sierra, la = mountain range
siete = seven
sigo: see *seguir (i)*
siguiente = following
silla, la = chair
sillón,el = armchair
simpático = kind, nice
sin embargo = however
sin gas = without gas, still (non-fizzy)
sino = but also
síntoma, el = symptom
sitio, el = place
situado = situated
sobre = above, on top of, on, about (of time)
sobre todo = especially
sofá, el = sofa
sois (from *ser*) = you (pl.) are
sol, el = sun
soleado = sunny
soler + infinitive = to be accustomed to do
    something – to 'normally' do
sólo = only
solomillo, el = sirloin
solucionar = to solve
sombrero, el = hat
somos (from *ser*) = we are
son (from *ser*) = they are; equals (=)
sonar = to ring (telephone)
sondeo, el = survey
sonido, el = sound
sopa de fideos, la = noodle soup
sopa, la = soup
soportar = to tolerate
sospechoso = suspicious
soy (from *ser*) = I am
squash, el = squash
su(s) = his/her/its/their (+ your, in polite form)
suave = mild
subir = to go up
subrayar = to underline

sucio = dirty
Sudamérica (fem.) = South America
Suecia (fem.) = Sweden
sueco = Swedish
suegra, la = mother-in-law
suegros, los = parents-in-law
suelo, el = floor
suelo: see *soler (ue)*
sueño, tener = to be sleepy
suficiente = sufficient, enough
superimportante = vital
supermercado, el = supermarket
sur, el = south
surf, el = surf
suspender = to fail (an examination)
tabla, la = plank, board, chart
tablón, el = notice-board
talla, la = size
taller, el = garage (mechanics)
tamaño, el = size
también = also, too
tampoco = neither
tan = so
tanto = so much
tapar = to cover
tapas , un bar de = a tapas bar
tapear = to have tapas
taquilla, la = box-office
tardar = to take one's time (to do something)
tarde = late
tarde, la = afternoon, early evening
tarjeta de crédito, la = credit card
tarta de queso, la = cheesecake
tauro = taurus
te = you, to you/ yourself
teatro, el = theatre
techo, el = ceiling
tecnología, la = technology
tejado, el = roof
tele, la = tv
telefonear = to telephone
telefónico = telephonic
teléfono, el = telephone
telenovela, la = tv soap-opera
televisión, la = television
temperatura, la = temperature
temprano = early
tener (ie) (1st person sing.: *tengo*) = to have, hold,
    consider; be (x years old)
tener buen tipo = to have a good figure
tener cuidado = to take care

tener enchufe = to have contacts
tener estilo = to have style, be fashionable
tener fiebre = to have a temperature
tener ganas de = to want to
tener prisa = to be in a hurry
tener que = to have to
tener que (+ infin.) = to have to, be obliged to
tener razón = to be right
tener sueño = to be tired/sleepy
tengo: from *tener* = I have
tengo muchas ganas = I really want
tenis, el = tennis
tercero = third
terminar = to finish
termómetro, el = thermometer
ternera, la = beef, veal
testigo, el = witness
ti (used after prepositions) = you, yourself
tía, la = aunt
tiempo, el = time, weather
tiempo lluvioso = rainy weather
tiempo soleado = sunny weather
tienda, la = shop
tiene(s): from *tener (ie)*
tierra, la = ground, earth
tijeras, las = scissors
tímido = timid
tinto = red (wine)
tío, el = uncle
típico = typical
tipo, el = person, type
tirando = so-so, not bad
título, el = title
tocar = to play (a musical instrument)
todavía = still, yet
todo = every, all
todo el mundo = everybody
todo recto = straight ahead
¡toma apuntes! = take notes!
tomar = to take (to have of meals)
tomar algo = to have a drink
tomar la alternativa = to become a matador
tomar nota = to take an order
tomate, el = tomato
tónica, la = tonic
torcer = to twist, turn
torear = to bullfight
tormenta, la = storm
toro, el = bull
toros, los = bullfight
tortilla, la = omelette

tortuga, la = tortoise
tostada, la = toast
tostado = toasted
tostador, el = toaster
trabajador = hardworking
trabajar = to work
trabajo, el = work
tradición, la = tradition
traducir = to translate
traer = to bring
traje de luces, el = bullfighter's costume
traje, el = suit
tranquilo = calm
tratar de = to try to
treinta = thirty
tremendo = awful, frightful
tres = three
trescientos = three hundred
triste = sad
tropical = tropical
tú = you (sing.)
tu(s) = your
turismo, el = tourism
turista, el/la = tourist
turrón, el = nougat
tutoría, la = tutorial
tuyo(s) = your(s)
últimamente = recently
un, una = a
un abrazo = with best wishes
único = only
uniforme, el = uniform
universidad, la = university
uno = one
unos = some, a few; about
Uruguay, el = Uruguay
usted (vd.), ustedes (vds.) = you (polite form)
usted verá = you will see
útil = useful
utilizar = to use
va (from *ir*) = he/she/it goes
vaca, la = cow
vacaciones, las = holidays
vago = lazy
¿vale? = ok?
valer = to be worth, to cost
válido (val.) = valid
valiente = brave, strong
*vamos (*from *ir)* = we go; let's go
vapor, el = steam
vaqueros, los = jeans

variado = varied
vario = assorted, various
vas (from *ir*) = you (sing.) go
vaso, el = glass
¡vaya! = what a shame!
vaya/vayan (from *ir*) = go!
vd., ud., usted = you (polite singular)
vds., uds., ustedes = you (polite plural)
ve (from *ir*) = go!
veces: (pl. of *vez*) = times
vecino, el/la = neighbour
vegetariano = vegetarian
veinte = twenty
vela, la = sailing
vencido, el = the loser
vender = to sell
Venezuela (fem.) = Venezuela
venga ¡venga! = come on!
ventana, la = window
ver = to see
verá (from *ver*) = he/she/it will see
veranear = to spend summer holidays
verano, el = summer
verbo, el = verb
verdad, la = truth
verdaderamente = really
verdadero = true
verde = green
verduras, las = vegetables, greens
vestíbulo, el = hall
vestido, el = dress
vestirse (i) = to get dressed
vez, la (pl.: *veces*) = time (occasion)
vía, la = way
viajar = to travel
viaje, el = journey
vida, la = life
vídeo, el = video

viejo = old
viento, el = wind
viernes = friday
vinagre, el = vinegar
vino, el = wine
virgo = virgo (star sign)
virus, el = virus
visitar = to visit
vista, la = sight, glance
visto: see *vestirse (i)*
vivir = to live
volar = to fly
voleibol, el = volley-ball
volver (ue) = to return
volverse loco = to go mad
vosotros/as = you (pl.)
voy (from *ir*) = i am going
vuelve: see *volver (ue)*
vuestro = your
wáter, el = lavatory
windsurfing, el = windsurfing
y = and
y cuarto = quarter past
y media = half past
y pico = about (with time)
ya = already
ya veremos = we will see
yo = i; (*soy yo* = it's me)
yo no sé = i don't know
yogur, el = yoghurt
zanahoria, la = carrot
zapatillas (de deporte), las = trainers
zapato, el = shoe
zona, la = zone, area
zoo, el = zoo
zumo, el = juice

Vocabulario: inglés-español

a = *un, una*
able, to be = *poder (ue)*
about (approximately) = *unos; sobre*
about (with time) = *y pico*
above = *arriba; sobre*
abroad = *al extranjero; extranjero*
academy = *academia, la*
accent = *acento, el*
accompany, to = *acompañar*
according to = *según*
ache = *dolor, el*
active = *activo*
activity = *actividad, la*
actor = *actor, el*
add, to = *añadir; echar; incorporar; agregar*
address = *dirección, la*
address book = *agenda, la*
adequate = *adecuado*
adjective = *adjetivo, el*
admit, to = *reconocer*
advice = *consejo, el*
affectionate = *cariñoso*
after = *después de*
afternoon = *tarde, la*
afternoon snack = *merienda, la*
afterwards = *después*
again = *otra vez*
age = *edad, la*
agreed! = *¡de acuerdo!*
agreement = *acuerdo, el*
agricultural = *agrario*
agriculture = *agricultura, la*
air-conditioning = *aire acondicionado, el*
all = *todo*
allow, to = *dejar; permitir*
almost = *casi*
along = *por*
alphabet = *alfabeto, el*
already = *ya*
also = *también*
always = *siempre*
America = *América* (fem.)
American = *americano*
amusing = *divertido*
anchovy = *boquerón, el*
and = *y; e* (before *i* and *hi*)

angry = *enfadado; furioso*
animal = *animal, el*
annoying = *pesado*
anorak = *anorak, el*
answer = *respuesta, la*
answer, to = *contestar*
anthropology = *antropología, la*
antibiotics = *antibióticos, los*
anxious = *nervioso*
anyhow = *de todas formas*
anything = *cualquier cosa*
anyway = *de todas formas*
apart = *aparte* (adverb)
appear, to = *parecer*
appearance = *físico, el*
apple = *manzana, la*
appropriate = *adecuado*
April = *abril* (masc.)
aquarius (star sign) = *acuario*
aquatic = *acuático*
area, zone = *zona, la*
Argentina = *Argentina* (fem.)
Argentinian = *argentino*
aries (star sign) = *aries*
arm = *brazo, el*
armchair = *butaca, la; sillón, el*
army = *ejército, el*
around (time) = *a eso de*
arrange to meet, to = *quedar*
arrival = *llegada, la*
arrive, to = *llegar*
art = *arte, el; dibujo, el*
article = *artículo, el*
as = *como*
as a general rule = *por regla general*
as a result = *como consecuencia*
as regards = *en cuanto a*
as soon as = *en cuanto*
ask (a question), to = *preguntar*
ask for, to = *pedir (i)*
aspirin = *aspirina, la*
assorted = *variado*
at = *a*
at any rate = *de todas formas*
at once = *en seguida*
athletics = *atletismo, el*

atmosphere = *ambiente, el*
August = *agosto* (masc.)
aunt = *tía, la*
Australia = *Australia* (fem.)
Australian = *australiano*
autumn = *otoño, el*
avoid, to = *evitar*
awful = *fatal*
back = *espalda, la*
bad = *malo* (*mal* before masc. sing. noun)
bad thing, the = *lo malo*
bad weather, it's = *hace mal tiempo, hace malo*
bag, purse = *bolso, el*
baker = *panadero, el*
bakery = *panadería, la*
balanced = *equilibrado*
banana = *plátano, el*
band, group = *grupo, el; banda, la*
bank = *banco, el*
bar = *bar, el*
barbarism = *barbaridad, la*
bargain = *ganga, la*
basin = *lavabo, el*
basketball = *baloncesto, el*
bath = *bañera, la*
bath, to have a = *bañarse*
bathroom = (*cuarto de*) *baño, el*
be, to = *estar; ser. Ser* is used for who or what something is (permanently); *estar* is used for where something is, or what something is (temporarily).
be called, to = *llamarse*
beach = *playa, la*
beat (mix), to = *batir*
because = *porque*
because of = *a causa de*
become, to = *hacerse* (irreg.)
bed = *cama, la*
bedroom = *dormitorio, el*
bedside table = *mesita de noche, la*
beef = *ternera, la*
beer = *cerveza, la*
before (with verb) = *antes de* (+ infin.)
begin, to = *comenzar (ie); empezar (ie)*
behind = *detrás de*
Belgian = *belga*
Belgium = *Bélgica* (fem.)
believe, to = *creer*
belt = *cinturón, el*
bench = *banco, el*
beret = *gorra, la*

besides = *además*
best wishes = *saludos*
best wishes, with = *un abrazo*
better, best = *mejor*
between = *entre*
bicycle = *bicicleta, la*
big = *grande*
bigger, biggest = *mayor*
bike = *bici, la* (abbreviation)
biology = *biología, la*
bird = *pájaro, el*
biro = *bolígrafo, el*
birth = *nacimiento, el*
birthday = *cumpleaños, el*
biscuit = *galleta, la*
bit, and a = *pico, y*
black = *negro*
blackboard = *pizarra, la*
blank = *hueco, el*
blonde = *rubio*
blouse = *blusa, la*
blue = *azul*
board = *tabla, la*
boat (small) = *barca, la*
body = *cuerpo, el*
boil, to = *hervir;* (an egg) *escalfar*
boiling hot, to be = *estar asado*
bon apetit! = *¡qué aproveche!*
book = *libro, el*
bookcase = *estantería, la*
boot = *bota, la*
border with, to = *limitar con*
bore = *rollo, el*
boring = *aburrido*
born, to be = *nacer*
bottle (little) = *botellín, el*
box-office = *taquilla, la*
boy = *chico, el;* child (male) *niño, el*
boyfriend = *novio, el*
brand = *marca, la*
brave = *valiente*
bread = *pan, el*
break = *recreo, el*
breakfast, to have = *desayunar*
breast (of chicken) = *pechuga, la*
bright = *claro*
brilliant = *fenomenal*
bring, to = *traer*
brochure = *folleto, el*
broken (down) = *estropeado*
brother = *hermano, el*

brown = *marrón*
brown sugar = *azúcar moreno, el*
brush one's teeth, to = *limpiarse los dientes*
build, to = *construir*
building = *edificio, el*
bull = *toro, el*
bullfight = *corrida de toros, la; corrida, la; toros, los*
bullfight, to = *lidiar; torear*
bullfighter (who kills the bull) = *matador, el*
bullfighter's costume = *traje de luces, el*
bullfighter's display/performance = *faena, la*
bullring = *plaza de toros, la*
bun = *bollo, el*
bus = *autobús, el*
bushy = *poblado*
but = *pero*
buy, to = *comprar*
by = *por*
café = *cafetería, la*
calculator = *calculadora, la*
calibre = *calibre, el*
call = *llamada, la*
called (surname), to be = *apellidarse*
calm = *tranquilo*
Canada = *Canadá* (masc.)
Canaries = *Canarias, las*
cancer (star sign) = *cáncer*
canteen = *cantina, la*
cap, beret = *gorra, la*
cape = *muleta, la*
capital (city) = *capital, la*
capricorn (star sign) = *capricornio*
car = *coche, el;* (travelling by) *en coche*
care = *cuidado, el*
caretaker = *conserje, el*
Caribbean = *el Caribe* (masc.)
carpet = *alfombra, la*
carrot = *zanahoria, la*
carry, to = *llevar*
cash (slang) = *pasta, la*
Castilian = *castellano*
castle = *castillo, el*
cat = *gato, el*
Catalan = *catalán*
cathedral = *catedral, la*
cauliflower = *coliflor, la*
cd, cd player = *compact disc, el*
ceiling = *techo, el*
celebrate, to = *celebrar*
celebrity, important person = *personaje, el*

central America = *Centroamérica* (fem.)
centre = *centro, el*
centre, in the = *céntrico*
cereals = *cereales, los*
certain = *seguro*
chair = *silla, la*
champagne = *cava, el*
champion = *campeón, el*
championship = *campeonato, el*
change, to = *cambiar*
change roles = *cambia de papel*
chapel = *capilla, la*
character = *personaje, el*
chart = *tabla, la*
chat, to = *charlar*
cheap = *barato*
cheese = *queso, el*
cheesecake = *tarta de queso, la*
chemist = *farmacéutico, el*
chemistry = *química, la*
chemists (shop) = *farmacia, la*
chess = *ajedrez, el*
chestnut-coloured = *castaño*
chicken = *pollo, el*
chickpea = *garbanzo, el*
child (male) = *niño, el*
Chile = *Chile* (masc.)
Chilean = *chileno*
chilly, it's = *hace fresco*
China = *China* (fem.)
Chinese = *chino*
chips = *patatas fritas, las*
chocolate = *chocolate, el*
choose, to = *elegir*
chop = *chuleta, la*
Christmas = *navidad, la*
Christmas Eve = *nochebuena, la*
church = *iglesia, la*
cider = *sidra, la*
cigarette = *cigarillo, el*
cinema = *cine, el*
city = *ciudad, la*
clam = *almeja, la*
class, classroom = *clase, la*
classical = *clásico*
classroom = *aula* (fem.)*, el*
clear = *despejado*
clear, bright = *claro*
clear, to be = *estar despejado*
climate = *clima, el*
clock = *reloj, el*

close, near (to) = *cerca (de)*
clothes = *ropa, la*
cloudy = *nublado*
cloudy, to be = *estar nublado*
club = *club, el*
coach = *autocar, el*
coast = *costa, la*
coat = *abrigo, el*
cocoa = *cacao, el*
coconut = *coco, el*
coffee (white) = *café (con leche), el*
coke = *coca cola, la*
cold, it's (very) = *hace (mucho) frío*
cold, to be = *hacer* frío
colour = *color, el*
Columbia = *Colombia* (fem.)
Columbian = *colombiano*
column = *columna, la*
comb one's hair, to = *peinarse*
come on! = *venga ¡venga!*
come on, come off it! = *¡anda!*
comfortable = *cómodo*
commentary = *comentario, el*
companion = *compañero/a, el/la*
compare, to = *comparar*
compass = *brújula, la*
complete = *completo*
complete, to = *completar*
compulsory = *obligatorio*
computer = *ordenador, el*
concert = *concierto, el*
consider, to = *considerar*
consist of, to = *consistir en*
contacts, to have = *tener enchufe*
container = *recipiente, el*
content, happy = *contento*
continue, to = *seguir (i)*(1st person sing. = *sigo*)
continuous = *continuo*
conversation = *conversación, la*
convince, to = *convencer*
cook = *cocinero, el*
cook, to = *cocer (ue)*
cook, to = *cocinar*
cooked in garlic = *al ajillo*
cool (colloquial) = *chulo*
cool (informal) = *guay*
cool, fresh = *fresco*
scool down, to = *refrescarse*
corner (of street/road) = *esquina, la*
correct = *correcto*
correct, to = *corregir (i)*

correspondent = *corresponsal, el*
corresponding = *correspondiente*
cost, to = *valer*
Costa Rica = *Costa Rica* (fem.)
cotton = *algodón, el*
count, to = *contar*
country = *país, el*
countryside = *campo, el*
countryside = *paisaje, el*
course (of meal) = *plato, el*
courtyard = *patio, el*
cousin (female) = *prima, la*
cousin (male) = *primo, el*
cover, to = *tapar*
cow = *vaca, la*
cravat = *corbata, la*
crazy = *loco*
crazy about, to be = *estar loco por*
crazy about, to be = *chiflar* (works like *gustar*)
cream = *nata, la*
credit card = *tarjeta de crédito, la*
crème caramel = *flan, el*
crop = *cultivo, el*
cross, to = *cruzar*
crown = *corona, la*
Cuban = *cubano*
cucumber = *pepino, el*
curiosity = *curiosidad, la*
curly = *rizado*
currency = *moneda, la*
cut, to = *cortar*
cycling = *ciclismo, el*
dad, daddy = *papá*
daily = *(a) diario*
dance, to = *bailar*
Danish = *danés*
dark (colour) = *moreno*
darling = *cariño*
date = *fecha, la*
daughter = *hija, la*
dawn = *madrugada, la*
day = *día, el*
day after tomorrow = *pasado mañana*
dear = *querido*
December = *diciembre* (masc.)
decide, to = *decidir*
degree = *grado, el*
degrees, it's x = *hace x grados*
delicious = *riquísimo; para chuparse los dedos*
Denmark = *Dinamarca* (fem.)
dental floss = *hilo dental, el*

department store = *grandes almacenes, los*
describe, to = *describir*
description = *descripción, la*
desk = *pupitre, el*
dessert, pudding = *postre, el*
detail = *detalle, el*
develop, to = *desarrollar*
diagnosis = *diagnóstico, el*
dialogue = *diálogo, el*
diary = *agenda, la*
dictionary = *diccionario, el*
diet = *dieta, la*
diet, to go on a = *ponerse a régimen*
different = *diferente*
dine, to = *cenar*
dining room = *comedor, el;* (canteen) *cantina, la*
dinner = *cena, la*
dirty = *sucio*
disciplined = *disciplinado*
disco = *discoteca, la*
discount = *descuento, el*
discover, to = *descubrir*
disgusting = *asqueroso*
dish, course = *plato, el*
dishwasher = *lavaplatos, el*
distraught, to be = *estar hecho polvo*
divide, to = *dividir*
divided = *dividido*
do, to = *hacer* (irreg.)
doctor = *médico, el*
dog = *perro, el*
dominoes = *dominó, el*
donkey = *burro, el*
don't be silly = *no seas tonto*
donut = *donut, el*
door = *puerta, la*
drain, to = *escurrir*
draw, to = *dibujar*
dress = *vestido, el*
dress (salads), to = *aliñar*
dressed, to get = *vestirse (i)*
dressing = *aliño, el*
drink = *bebida, la*
drink, to = *beber;* (to have a) *tomar algo*
drop off, to = *dejar*
drops of, a few = *chorrito, un*
drugs = *drogas, las*
dry = *seco*
dual-carriageway = *autovía, la*
during = *durante*
Dutch = *holandés*

each = *cada*
ear = *oreja, la*
early = *temprano*
early morning = *madrugada, la*
earring = *pendiente, el*
easily = *fácilmente*
east = *este, el*
easy = *fácil*
eat, to = *comer*
economy = *economía, la*
Ecuador = *Ecuador* (masc.)
Edinburgh = *Edimburgo* (masc.)
effort = *esfuerzo, el*
egg = *huevo, el;* (with stuffing) *huevo relleno, el*
eight = *ocho*
eight hundred = *ochocientos*
eighteen = *dieciocho*
eighth = *octavo*
eighty = *ochenta*
El Salvador = *El Salvador* (masc.)
elbow = *codo, el*
eleven = *once*
e-mail = *correo electrónico, el; emilio, el* (slang)
end = *fin, el; final, el*
end of, at the = *al fin de*
England = *Inglaterra* (fem.)
English (the nationality) = *inglés*
English (the language) = *inglés, el*
enjoy, to = *disfrutar*
enjoy your meal! = *¡que aproveche!*
enough = *bastante; suficiente*
enough (sufficient), to be = *bastar*
enter, to = *entrar*
entertaining = *entretenido*
equal = *igual*
equals (=) = *son* (from *ser*)
escape, to = *escaparse*
especially = *especialmente; sobre todo*
ethics = *ética, la*
euro = *euro, el*
even = *incluso*
evening = *tarde, la*
every = *cada; todo*
everybody = *todo el mundo*
exactly = *exactamente*
exam = *examen, el*
example = *ejemplo, el*
except = *menos*
except (for) = *excepto*
exchange = *intercambio, el*
exciting = *emocionante*

excuse me = *oiga; perdone*
exercise = *ejercicio, el*
exercise, to do = *hacer ejercicio*
exercise book = *cuaderno, el*
exotic = *exótico*
explain, to = *explicar*
explosive = *explosivo, el*
extrovert = *extrovertido; marchoso*
eye = *ojo, el*
eye-brow = *ceja, la*
face = *cara, la*
fail (an examination), to = *suspender*
fair, market = *feria, la*
fair-skinned = *rubio*
fall, to = *caer*
false = *falso*
family = *familia, la*
famous = *famoso*
fan, supporter = *aficionado, el*
fantastic = *fantástico*
far (from) = *lejos (de)*
farm = *granja, la*
fashionable = *de moda*
fashionable, to be = *tener estilo*
fat = *gordo*
father = *padre, el*
fatty foods = *comida grasa, la*
favourite = *favorito; preferido*
fear = *miedo, el*
February = *febrero*
fed up, to be = *estar harto*
feel good/bad, to = *encontrarse bien/mal*
feel, to = *sentirse*
feel like, to = *apetecer*
festival = *fiesta, la*
few, a = *unos*
field = *campo, el*
fifteen = *quince*
fifth = *quinto*
fifty = *cincuenta*
file, folder = *carpeta, la*
fill, to = *empastar*
fill in, to = *rellenar*
fillet = *filete, el*
film = *película, la*
find, to = *encontrar (ue)*
find out, to = *investigar*
fine weather, it's = *hace buen tiempo, hace bueno*
finger = *dedo, el*
finish, to = *terminar*
Finland = *Finlandia* (fem.)

Finnish = *finlandés*
first = *primero* (*primer* before masc. sing. noun)
first course (of meal) = *primer plato, el*
fish = *pescado, el; pez, el* (plural *peces*)
fit, to get = *ponerse en forma*
five = *cinco*
five hundred = *quinientos*
fix, to = *arreglar*
fizzy = *con gas*
flat (appartment) = *piso, el*
flip-flops = *chanclas, las*
floor = *piso, el; suelo, el;* (of apartment building) *planta, la*
flower = *flor, la*
flowery = *florido*
fly, to = *volar*
fog = *niebla, la*
foggy, it's = *hay niebla*
folder = *carpeta, la*
follow, continue, to = *seguir (i)*(1st person sing. = *sigo*)
following = *siguiente*
food = *comida, la*
foot = *pie, el*
football = *fútbol, el;* indoor (5-a-side) *fútbol sala, el*
for = *para; por*
for example = *por ejemplo*
for the first time = *por primera vez*
for the time being = *de momento*
foreign = *extranjero*
foreigner = *extranjero, el*
forget, to = *olvidar*
form = *ficha, la*
forty = *cuarenta*
four = *cuatro*
four hundred = *cuatrocientos*
fourteen = *catorce*
fourth = *cuarto*
France = *Francia* (fem.)
free = *libre*
freezer = *congelador, el*
French (nationality) = *francés*
French (language) = *francés, el*
frequency = *frecuencia, la*
fresh = *fresquito*
Friday = *viernes*
fridge = *nevera, la*
friend = *amigo, el; amiga, la*
from = *de; desde*
from time to time = *de vez en cuando*

frost = *escarcha, la*
frosty, it's = *hay escarcha*
frozen = *helado*
fruit = *fruta, la*
full = *lleno*
fun, funny = *divertido; gracioso*
furniture = *muebles, los*
fussy = *especial*
galaxy = *galaxia, la*
game = *juego, el;* (match) *partido, el*
games, sports = *deportes, los*
gap = *hueco, el*
garage (mechanics) = *taller, el*
garden = *jardín, el*
garlic = *ajo, el*
garnish = *guarnición, la*
gas = *gas, el*
gate (iron) = *cancela, la*
gemini = *géminis*
general = *general*
generally = *en general*
generous = *generoso*
geography = *geografía, la*
German = *alemán*
Germany = *Alemania* (fem.)
get, to = *conseguir*
get on well/badly with, to = *llevarse bien/fatal con*
get on with, to = *entenderse; llevarse*
get ready, to = *arreglarse*
get undressed, to = *quitarse la ropa*
get up, to = *levantarse*
girl = *chica, la;* child (female) *niña, la*
girlfriend = *novia, la*
give (as a present), to = *regalar*
give, to = *dar*
glass = *copa, la; vaso, el*
glasses (spectacles) = *gafas, las*
glove = *guante, el*
go, to = *ir* (irreg)
go down, to = *bajar*
go in, to = *entrar*
go out with, to = *salir con*
go out, to = *salir*
go to bed, to = *acostarse (ue)*
go up, to = *subir*
gold (the metal) = *oro, el*
golden, gold-coloured = *dorado*
golf = *golf, el*
good = *bueno* (*buen* before masc. sing. noun)
good afternoon = *buenas tardes*
good at, to be = *ser fuerte en*

good morning = *buenos días*
good night = *buenas noches*
good thing, the = *lo bueno*
good time, to have a = *pasarlo bien*
goodbye = *adiós*
good-natured = *feliz*
gram = *gramo, un*
grand-daughter = *nieta, la*
grandfather = *abuelo, el*
grandmother = *abuela, la*
grandson = *nieto, el*
grass = *hierba, la*
great (superb) = *estupendo; genial; magnífico*
great time, to have a = *pasarlo bomba*
Greece = *Grecia* (fem.)
Greek = *griego*
green = *verde*
green bean = *judía verde, la*
greetings = *saludos*
grey = *gris*
grill = *parrilla, la*
ground, earth = *tierra, la*
group (band) = *banda, la; grupo, el*
Guatemala = *Guatemala* (fem.)
guess, to = *adivinar*
guitar = *guitarra, la*
gulf = *golfo, el*
gymnastics = *gimnasia, la*
habit = *costumbre, la*
hair = *pelo, el*
hake (fish) = *merluza, la*
half = *medio*
half past = *y media*
hall = *vestíbulo, el*
ham = *jamón, el*
hamburger = *hamburguesa, la*
hammock = *hamaca, la*
hamster = *hámster, el*
hand = *mano, la*
handball = *balonmano, el*
handsome = *guapo*
happy = *alegre; contento;* (good-natured) *feliz*
hardworking = *trabajador*
harm, to = *perjudicar*
hat = *sombrero, el*
have, to = *tener (ie)* (1st person sing. = *tengo*);
    (possess) *poseer*
have a good figure, to = *tener buen tipo*
have a good trip! = *¡buen viaje!*
have lunch, to = *almorzar (ue)*
have to, to = *tener que* (+ infin.)

he = *él*
head = *cabeza, la*
headteacher = *director, el; directora, la*
health = *salud, la*
healthy = *sano*
heat = *calor, el*
height, to be of a certain = *medir (i)*
helicopter = *helicóptero, el*
hello = *buenos días; hola; dígame*
help, to = *ayudar*
her = *su(s)*
here = *aquí*
hi there = *muy buenas*
highest = *máximo*
hiking = *footing, el*
him, to him = *le*
himself/herself = *se*
hip = *cadera, la*
his = *su(s)*
Hispanic, Spanish = *hispano*
history = *historia, la*
hobby = *pasatiempo, el; afición, la*
hold, to = *tener (ie)* (1st person sing. = *tengo*)
holidays = *vacaciones, las*
Holland = *Holanda* (fem.)
Holy Week (Easter) = *semana santa, la*
homework = *deberes, los*
homework, to do one's = *hacer los deberes*
Honduras = *Honduras* (fem.)
horoscope = *horóscopo, el*
horrible = *antipático; horrible*
horse = *caballo, el*
hospital = *hospital, el*
hot = *caliente*
hot, it's (very) = *hace (mucho) calor*
hotel = *hotel, el*
hour = *hora, la*
house = *casa, la*
housewife = *ama* (fem.) *de casa, el*
how? = *¿cómo?*
how are you? = *¿qué tal?*
how delicious! = *¡qué rico!*
how disgusting! = *¡qué asco!*
how do I get to? = *¿por dónde se va a?*
how exciting! = *¡qué ilusión!*
how extraordinary! = *¡qué barbaridad!*
how lucky! = *¡qué suerte!*
how much? how many? = *¿cuánto/a/os/as?*
how nice! = *¡qué gusto!*
how scary! = *¡qué miedo!*
how strange! = *¡qué raro!*

however = *sin embargo*
how's it going? = *¿qué hay?*
hug = *abrazo, el*
hundred = *cien(to)*
hunger = *hambre* (fem.), *el*
hurry, to be in a = *tener prisa*
hurt, to = *doler*
husband = *marido, el*
I = *yo*
I am = *soy* (from *ser*)
I.D. card = *carné de indentidad, el*
i.e./ that's to say = *o sea*
ice = *hielo, el*
ice-cream = *helado, el; mantecado, el*
ICT = *informática, la*
icy, it's = *hay hielo*
idol = *ídolo, el*
if = *si*
illustrated = *ilustrado*
imperative = *imperativo, el*
important = *importante*
impression = *impresión, la*
improve, to = *mejorar*
in = *en*
in fact = *de hecho*
in front of = *delante de*
in my judgement = *a mi juicio*
in my opinion = *en mi opinión*
in order to = *para* (+ infin.); *por* (+ infin.)
in total = *en total*
in x minutes' time = *dentro de x minutos*
incredible = *increíble*
Indian = *indio*
infinitive = *infinitivo, el*
inflamed = *inflamado*
information = *información, la*
ingredient = *ingrediente, el*
inhabitant = *habitante, el/la*
inhuman = *inhumano*
instead of = *en lugar de; en vez de*
instruction = *instrucción, la*
intelligent = *inteligente*
interest, to = *interesar*
interesting = *interesante*
interview = *entrevista, la*
interview, to = *entrevistar*
invent, to = *inventar*
Ireland = *Irlanda* (fem.)
Irish = *irlandés*
iron = *hierro, el*
ironed = *planchado*

island = *isla, la*
issued = *expedido (esped.)*
it (direct object pronoun) = *lo*
Italian = *italiano*
Italy = *Italia* (fem.)
its = *su(s)*
jacket = *chaqueta, la*
January = *enero* (masc.)
Japan = *Japón* (masc.)
Japanese = *japonés*
jar = *jarra, la*
jeans = *vaqueros, los*
jogging, to go = *hacer footing*
joking, you must be! = *¡no fastidies!*
journey = *viaje, el*
juice = *zumo, el*
July = *julio* (masc.)
June = *junio* (masc.)
just = *justo*
keep fit, to = *mantenerse en forma*
kill, to = *matar*
kilometre = *kilómetro, el*
kind = *simpático*
king = *rey, el*
kitchen = *cocina, la*
kiwi = *kiwi, el*
knee = *rodilla, la*
know (a person or place), to = *conocer*
know, to = *saber*
laboratory = *laboratorio, el*
lamb = *cordero, el*
lamp = *lámpara, la*
landscape = *paisaje, el*
language = *idioma, el; lengua, la*
lasagne = *lasaña, la*
last, to = *durar*
late = *tarde*
later = *luego*
Latin = *latín, el*
lavatory = *wáter, el*
lawyer = *abogado, el*
lazy = *perezoso; vago*
learn, to = *aprender*
leather = *cuero, el*
leave, to = *dejar*
left = *izquierda*
leg = *pierna, la*
lemon = *limón, el*
lend, to = *prestar*
leo (star sign) = *leo*
less = *menos*

let's go = *vamos (*from *ir)*
let's see whether, let's hope that = *a ver si*
letter (correspondence) = *carta, la*
lettuce = *lechuga, la*
libra (star sign) = *libra*
library = *biblioteca, la*
lie = *mentira, la*
lie, to tell a = *mentir (ie)*
life = *vida, la*
light (noun) = *luz, la* (pl. *luces*)
light (adj.) = *ligero*
lightning = *rayo, el*
like = *como*
like, to = *gustar*
like that = *así*
likewise = *igualmente*
lion = *león, el*
listen, to = *escuchar*
literature = *literatura, la*
little (amount) = *poco*
live, to = *vivir*
living room = *sala de estar, la; salón, el*
loads of = *montón de, un*
location = *localidad, la*
lock = *cerradura, la*
lock up, to = *encerrar*
London = *Londres* (masc.)
long = *largo*
look at, to = *mirar*
look for, to = *buscar*
lose, to = *perder (ie)*
lose weight, to = *adelgazar*
loser = *vencido, el*
love, to = *encantar; chiflar* (both verbs work like *gustar*)
loving = *cariñoso*
low = *bajo*
lunch = *almuerzo, el; comida, la*
luxury, high class = *de lujo*
mad, to go = *volverse loco*
magazine = *revista, la*
main = *principal*
main course (of meal) = *segundo plato, el*
maintenance = *mantenimiento, el*
make, to = *hacer* (irreg.)
make sense, to = *sentido, tener*
man = *hombre, el*
mandarine = *mandarina, la*
map = *mapa, el*
March = *marzo* (masc.)
marker pen = *rotulador, el*

market = *mercado, el*
market, fair = *feria, la*
married = *casado*
martyr = *mártir, el/la*
martyr, to = *martirizar*
marzipan = *mazapán, el*
mass = *misa, la*
matador, to become a = *tomar la alternativa*
match up, to = *emparejar*
match, game = *partido, el*
maths = *matemáticas, las*
matter, it doesn't = *no importa*
May = *mayo* (masc.)
maybe = *quizá(s)*
mayonnaise = *mayonesa, la*
me, to me = *me*
meal = *comida, la*
meat = *carne, la*
meatball = *albóndiga, la*
medicine = *medicamento, el*
medium (cooked) = *medio hecho*
meet, to = *encontrar (ue); recoger*
melon = *melón, el*
mention, to = *mencionar*
metre = *metro, el*
metro (underground train system) = *metro, el*
Mexican = *mejicano (mexicano)*
Mexico = *México (Méjico)* (masc.)
mild = *suave*
milk = *leche, la*
milkshake = *batido, el*
million = *millón, el*
mime = *mimo, el*
mine = *mina, la*
mineral = *mineral*
mining (noun) = *minería, la*
mining (adj.) = *minero*
miniskirt = *minifalda, la*
minus (-) = *menos*
minute = *minuto, el*
mirror = *espejo, el*
Miss = *señorita*
miss (a person/place), to = *echar de menos*
mix, to = *mezclar;* (whisk) *batir*
mixed (adj.) = *mixto*
mobile telephone = *móvil, el*
modern = *moderno*
molar = *muela, la*
moment = *momento, el*
Monday = *lunes*
money = *dinero, el*

month = *mes, el*
more = *más*
more and more = *cada vez más*
morning = *mañana, la*
most = *más*
mother = *madre, la*
mother-in-law = *suegra, la*
motorcycling = *motociclismo, el*
mountain = *montaña, la*
mountain range = *sierra, la*
mouse = *ratón, el*
mouth = *boca, la*
mouthwash = *enjuague, el*
Mr = *señor*
Mrs = *señora*
much, many = *mucho*
multiplied = *multiplicado*
multiply, to = *multiplicar*
mum, mummy = *mamá*
municipal = *municipal*
muscle = *músculo, el*
museum = *museo, el*
mushroom = *champiñón, el*
music = *música, la*
mussel = *mejillón, el*
must, to = *deber*
mustard = *mostaza, la*
my = *mi(s)*
name = *nombre, el*
nationality = *nacionalidad, la*
nativity scene = *belén, el*
natural = *natural;* (normal) *normal*
navy blue = *azul marino*
near (adj.) = *cercano*
near (to) = *cerca (de)*
necessary = *necesario*
necessary, to be = *hacer falta*
neck = *cuello, el*
neck-tie = *corbata, la*
neighbour = *vecino, el/la*
neither = *tampoco*
neither…nor = *ni…ni*
nervous = *nervioso*
never = *nunca*
new = *nuevo*
New Year's Eve = *nochevieja, la*
newspaper = *periódico, el*
next = *próximo;* (that is coming) *que viene*
next to = *al lado de*
next year = *año que viene, el*
Nicaragua = *Nicaragua* (fem.)

nice = *simpático*
nickname = *apodo, el*
night = *noche, la*
nine = *nueve*
nine hundred = *novecientos*
nineteen = *diecinueve*
ninety = *noventa*
ninth = *noveno*
no = *no;* (not any) *ninguno* (*ningún* before masc. sing. noun)
no way! = *¡qué va! ¡ni hablar!*
nocilla (a type of chocolate spread) = *nocilla, la*
noisy = *ruidoso*
noodle = *fideo, el*
normal = *normal*
normally = *normalmente*
normally do, to = *soler* + infinitive
north = *norte, el*
Norway = *Noruega* (fem.)
Norwegian = *noruego*
nose = *nariz, la*
not = *no*
not at all, it's my pleasure = *de nada*
note = *apunte, el*
nothing = *nada*
notice of, to take = *fijarse en*
notice-board = *tablón, el*
nougat = *turrón, el*
November = *noviembre* (masc.)
now = *ahora*
nowadays = *hoy en día*
nowhere = *ninguna parte*
nuisance = *fastidio, el*
number = *número, el*
numerous = *numeroso*
o'clock = *en punto*
obey, to = *obedecer*
obsessed = *obsesionado*
obsessive (about), to become = *obsesionarse (con)*
ocean = *océano, el*
October = *octubre*
odd job = *chapuza, la*
of = *de*
of course = *claro; desde luego; por supuesto*
office = *oficina, la*
official = *oficial*
often = *a menudo*
oil (cooking) = *aceite, el*
oil (petroleum) = *petróleo, el*
ok? = *¿vale?*

okay; so, so = *regular*
old = *viejo*
older, oldest = *mayor*
olive = *aceituna, la*
omelette = *tortilla, la*
on = *en; sobre*
on average = *de media*
on foot = *andando*
on sale, to be = *estar de rebajas*
on the….hand side = *a mano…*
on the dot (of time) = *en punto*
on the point of, to be = *estar a punto de*
on the way = *de camino*
on the way to = *camino de*
on top of = *sobre*
one = *uno*
one has to = *hay que*
onion = *cebolla, la*
only = *sólo; único*
only child (male) = *hijo único, el;* (female) *hija única, la*
open, to = *abrir*
opposite (to) = *enfrente (de)*
optional = *optativo*
or = *o*
oral hygiene = *higiene bucal, la*
orange (the colour) = *naranja*
orange (the fruit) = *naranja, la*
order = *orden, el*
order, to = *mandar*
order, to take an = *tomar nota*
oregano = *orégano, el*
origin = *origen, el*
other = *otro*
ought (must), to = *deber*
our = *nuestro*
ourselves = *nos*
outgoing, extrovert = *extrovertido*
outside = *fuera*
outskirts = *afueras, las*
oven = *horno, el*
overcoat = *abrigo, el*
P.E. (physical education) = *educación física, la*
p.o. box = *apartado postal* (*apdo. postal*), *el*
Pacific = *Pacífico, el*
paella = *paella, la*
pagan = *pagano*
page = *página, la*
pain = *dolor, el; pena, la*
painted = *pintado*
painter = *pintor, el*

painting = *cuadro, el*

pair = *pareja, la*

Panama = *Panamá* (masc.)

paper; piece of paper = *papel, el*

paragraph = *párrafo, el*

Paraguay = *Paraguay* (masc.)

parent = *padre, el*

parents-in-law = *suegros, los*

park = *parque, el*

partner = *pareja, la*

party, festival = *fiesta, la*

pass (an examination), to = *aprobar (ue)*

pasta = *pasta, la*

pastime = *afición, la*

pastimes = *diversiones, las*

patriotic = *patriótico*

patron = *patrona, la*

pay for someone else, to = *invitar*

pear = *pera, la*

pedestrian = *peatón, el*

peel, to = *pelar*

pen, biro = *bolígrafo, el; boli, el* (abbreviation)

pencil = *lápiz, el*

pencil-case = *estuche, el*

pencil sharpener = *sacapuntas, el*

peninsula = *península, la*

pen-pal = *corresponsal, el*

people = *gente, la* (used in singular)

pepper = *pimiento, el*

per cent = *por ciento*

perfect = *perfecto*

perform, to = *actuar*

perhaps = *quizá(s)*

period, time = *época, la*

person = *persona, la*

person = *tipo, el*

Peru = *Perú* (masc.)

peso (unit of currency in some S. American countries) = *peso, el*

pet = *animal, el; mascota, la*

petroleum = *petróleo, el*

physics = *física, la*

picture = *imagen, la; dibujo, el*

piles of = *montón de, un*

pill = *pastilla, la*

pinch (e.g. of salt) = *pizca, una*

pineapple = *piña, la*

pink = *rosa*

pisces (star sign) = *piscis*

pizza = *pizza, la*

place = *sitio, el*

plan = *plano, el*

planet = *planeta, el*

plank = *tabla, la*

plaque = *caries, la*

play, to = *jugar*

play (a musical instrument), to = *tocar*

play a record, to = *poner un disco*

playground = *patio, el*

playing card = *carta, la*

pleasant = *agradable*

please = *por favor*

pleased (to meet you) = *encantado (de conocerte)*

plus (+) = *más*

poach (an egg), to = *escalfar*

point out, to = *indicar*

policeman = *policía, el*

polite = *educado*

poor = *pobre*

pop (short for popular) = *pop*

popular = *popular*

pork = *cerdo, el*

Portugal = *Portugal* (masc.)

Portugese = *portugués*

position = *posición, la*

post, to = *echar*

post office = *correos*

poster = *póster, el*

potato = *patata, la*

practise (do), to = *practicar*

prawn = *gamba, la*

pray, to = *orar ; rezar*

praying mantis = *mantis religiosa, la*

prefer, to = *preferir (ie)*

preparation = *elaboración, la*

prepare, to = *preparar*

prepare oneself, get ready, to = *prepararse*

present = *regalo, el*

present (adj.) = *presente*

present (tense) = *presente, el*

present, to = *presentar*

pretty = *bonito; guapo*

primary = *primario*

private = *privado*

probably = *a lo mejor*

problem = *problema, el*

produce, to = *producir*

producer = *productor, el*

programme = *programa, el*

projector = *proyector, el*

pronoun = *pronombre, el*

pronounce, to = *pronunciar*

province = *provincia, la*
prune = *pasa, la*
PSHE = *etica, la*
pudding = *postre, el*
pupil = *alumno/a, el/la*
purple = *morado*
purse = *bolso, el*
push, to = *empujar*
put, to = *meter; poner;* (place) *colocar*
put on, to = *ponerse*
put on weight, to = *engordar*
put up with, to = *aguantar*
pyramid = *pirámide, la*
quarter = *cuarto, el*
quarter past = *y cuarto*
quarter to = *menos cuarto*
queen = *reina, la*
question = *pregunta, la*
quick, quickly = *rápido; pronto*
quiet, to be = *callarse*
quite = *bastante*
rabbit = *conejo, el*
radio = *radio, la*
rain = *precipitaciones, las*
rain, to = *llover (ue)*
rainy = *lluvioso*
rainy weather = *tiempo lluvioso*
rare (cooked) = *poco hecho*
rarely = *frecuencia, con poca*
reach the age of, to = *cumplir*
reach, to = *alcanzar*
read, to = *leer*
reading = *lectura, la*
real = *real*
realise, to = *darse cuenta de*
really = *verdaderamente*
reason = *razón, la*
receive, to = *recibir*
recently = *últimamente*
recipe = *receta, la*
red = *rojo;* (of wine) *tinto*
redhead = *pelirrojo*
reduction = *rebaja, la*
reflexive = *reflexivo*
region = *región, la*
register, to take the = *pasar lista*
relax, to = *relajarse*
relaxed = *relajado*
Religious Studies (R.E.) = *religión, la*
remain, to = *quedar*
remember, to = *acordarse (ue)*

represented = *representado*
research, to = *investigar*
residence = *domicilio, el*
responsible = *responsable*
rest, to = *descansar*
restaurant = *restaurante, el*
return, to = *regresar; volver (ue)*
revision = *repaso, el*
rice = *arroz, el*
rice-pudding = *arroz con leche, el*
ride a bike, to = *montar en bici(cleta)*
riding (horse) = *equitación, la*
riding (horse), to go = *montar a caballo*
right = *derecho*
right, to be = *tener razón*
right away = *seguida, en; ahora mismo*
ring (telephone), to = *sonar*
road = *carretera, la*
roast/roasted = *asado*
roof = *tejado, el*
roof-rack = *baca, la*
room = *cuarto, el; habitación, la; sala, la*
rosé (wine) = *rosado*
rough = *rudo*
round = *redondo*
routine = *rutina, la*
royal = *real*
rubber = *goma, la*
rucksack = *mochila, la*
rugby = *rugby, el*
rule = *regla, la*
ruler = *regla, la*
rum = *ron, el*
run, to = *correr*
run under water, to = *pasar por agua*
Russia = *Rusia* (fem.)
Russian = *ruso*
sad = *triste*
sagittarius (star sign) = *sagitario*
sailing = *vela, la*
sailing, to go = *hacer vela; navegar*
sailor = *navegante, el*
saint = *santo, el*
salad = *ensalada, la*
salad bowl = *ensaladera, la*
sale, reduction = *rebaja, la*
salmon = *salmón, el*
salt = *sal, la*
same = *igual; mismo*
same as = *igual que*
sandal = *sandalia, la*

sandwich = *bocadillo, el*
Saturday = *sábado*
sausage (red spicy) = *chorizo, el; salchichón, el*
sauté, to = *rehogar*
say, to = *decir (i);* 1st person singular *digo*
scarf = *bufanda, la*
school = *escuela, la; cole, el* (shortened form);
    (primary) *colegio, el;* (secondary) *instituto, el*
school, of a = *escolar* (adj.)
school-bag = *mochila, la*
science = *ciencias, las*
scissors = *tijeras, las*
scorpion (star sign) = *escorpio*
Scotland = *Escocia* (fem.)
Scottish = *escocés*
scrub, to = *fregar (ie)*
sea = *mar, el*
sea bass = *lubina, la*
sea bream = *besugo, el*
season = *estación, la*
second = *segundo*
second course, as a = *de segundo*
secondary education = *educación secundaria
    obligatoria, la*
secretary = *secretaria, la*
sector = *sector, el*
see you later = *hasta la vista; hasta luego*
see, to = *ver*
seem, to = *parecer*
selfish = *egoísta*
sell, to = *vender*
send, to = *mandar*
sense = *sentido, el*
sentence = *frase, la*
September = *se(p)tiembre*
serve, to = *atender*
seven = *siete*
seven hundred = *setecientos*
seventeen = *diecisiete*
seventh = *séptimo*
seventy = *setenta*
shack = *chabola, la*
shandy = *clara, la*
shape = *forma, la*
shave, to = *afeitarse*
she = *ella*
shellfish = *marisco, el*
shirt = *camisa, la;* (short-sleeved sports) *camiseta
    polo, la*
shoe = *zapato, el*
shoe size, to be of a certain = *calzar*

shop = *tienda, la*
shop assistant = *dependienta, la*
shopping = *compra, la*
shopping, to do the = *hacer la compra; ir de
    tiendas, ir de compras*
short (height) = *bajo*
short (length) = *corto*
shoulder = *hombro, el*
show, to = *enseñar*
show (a film), to = *poner*
shower = *ducha, la*
shower, to have a = *ducharse*
showers = *chubascos, los*
showing/screening = *sesión, la*
shut, lock up, to = *encerrar*
side = *lado, el*
sight, glance = *vista, la*
silver (the colour) = *plateado*
silver (the metal) = *plata, la*
similar = *parecido*
simmer, to let = *dejar cocer a fuego suave*
since, because = *puesto que*
sink = *fregadero, el*
sirloin = *solomillo, el*
sister = *hermana, la*
sit down, to = *sentarse (ie)*
situated = *situado*
sit-up = *abdominal, el*
six = *seis*
six hundred = *seiscientos*
sixteen = *dieciséis*
sixth = *sexto*
sixty = *sesenta*
size = *talla, la; tamaño, el*
skate, to = *patinar*
skating = *patinaje, el*
ski, to = *esquiar*
ski resort = *estación de esquí, la*
skiing = *esquí, el*
skilful = *hábil*
skin = *piel, la*
ski-pass = *forfait, el*
skirt = *falda, la*
ski-slope = *pista de esquí, la*
ski-stick = *bastón, el*
sky = *cielo, el*
sleep, to = *dormir (ue)*
sleepy, to be = *sueño, tener*
slice = *rodaja, la*
slim = *delgado*
slow = *lento; despacio*

small = *pequeño*
smaller = *menor*
smoke, to = *fumar*
snack, to have a = *merendar (ie)*
snow = *nieve, la*
snow, to = *nevar (ie)*
so = *tan*
so (then) = *así que*
so much = *tanto*
soap = *jabón, el*
soap-opera = *telenovela, la; culebrón, el*
sock = *calcetín, el*
sofa = *sofá, el*
soft drink = *refresco, el*
sole (fish) = *lenguado, el*
solve, to = *solucionar*
some = *algún, alguna; unos*
something = *algo*
sometimes = *a veces; algunas veces*
son = *hijo, el*
sorrow = *pena, la*
sorry, I am = *lo siento*
so-so, not bad = *tirando*
sound = *sonido, el*
soup = *sopa, la*
south = *sur, el*
South America = *Sudamérica* (fem.)
southern = *meridional*
spaghetti = *espaguetis, los*
Spain = *España* (fem.)
Spanish = *español*
Spanish (language) = *español, el*
speak, to = *hablar*
speak on the telephone, to = *hablar por teléfono*
special = *especial*
spectacle = *espectáculo, el*
speech = *discurso, el*
spell out, to = *deletrear*
spend (money), to = *gastar*
spider = *araña, la*
spinach = *espinacas, las*
sport = *deporte, el*
sports centre, sports hall = *polideportivo, el*
sporty = *deportista; deportivo*
spring (the season) = *primavera, la*
square (of a town) = *plaza, la*
squash = *squash, el*
squid = *calamar, el*
stadium = *estadio, el*
staff room = *sala de profesores, la*
stand (tolerate), to = *aguantar*

start, to = *empezar (ie)*
station = *estación, la*
stay = *estancia, la*
stay, to = *quedarse*
stay at home, to = *quedarse en casa*
steam = *vapor, el*
step-brother = *hermanastro, el*
step-father = *padrastro, el*
step-mother = *madrastra, la*
step-sister = *hermanastra, la*
stereotype = *estereotipo, el*
stew = *cocido, el*
still (non-fizzy) = *sin gas*
still, yet = *todavía*
sting, to = *picar*
stir, to = *remover*
stockings = *medias, las*
storm = *tormenta, la*
stormy, it's = *hay tormenta*
story = *historia, la*
straight = *recto;* (hair) *liso*
straight ahead = *todo recto*
strange, odd = *raro*
street = *calle, la*
strong = *fuerte; valiente*
student = *estudiante, el/la*
study, to = *estudiar*
stuff oneself, to = *inflarse de comer*
stupid = *imbécil*
subject (school) = *asignatura, la*
success, to be a = *ser un éxito*
suck, to = *chupar*
suckling pig = *cochinillo, el*
sugar = *azúcar, el*
sugar cane = *caña de azúcar, la*
suit = *traje, el*
suit, (go with), to = *pegar con; sentar*
summer = *verano, el*
summer holidays, to spend = *veranear*
sun = *sol, el*
Sunday = *domingo*
sunglasses = *gafas de sol, las*
sunny = *soleado*
sunny, it's = *hace sol*
superb = *estupendo; magnífico;* (informal) *guay*
supermarket = *supermercado, el*
supporter = *aficionado, el*
sure = *seguro*
sure, to be = *estar seguro*
surf = *surf, el*
surf (e.g. the internet), to = *navegar*

surname = *apellido, el*
surprise, to = *extrañar*
survey = *encuesta, la; sondeo, el*
suspicious = *sospechoso*
swap around = *cambia de papel*
Sweden = *Suecia* (fem.)
Swedish = *sueco*
sweet = *dulce*
sweets = *chucherías, las (chuches)*
swim, to = *nadar*
swimmer = *nadador, el*
swimming = *natación, la*
swimming costume = *bañador, el*
swimming pool = *piscina, la*
sword = *espada, la*
symptom = *síntoma, el*
table = *mesa, la*
tacky = *hortera*
take, to = *coger; tomar;* (buy) *llevarse*
take care, to = *tener cuidado*
take notes! = *toma apuntes ¡toma apuntes!*
take off, remove, to = *quitar*
take one's time (to do something), to = *tardar*
take out, to = *sacar*
tall = *alto*
tapas, to have = *tapear*
tapas bar = *bar de tapas, el*
tape = *cinta, la*
taste = *gusto, el; sabor, el*
tasty = *rico; sabroso*
tasty, to be = *estar bueno*
taurus = *tauro*
teach, to = *enseñar*
teacher = *profesor, el; profesora, la*
team = *equipo, el; partido, el; cuadrilla, la*
teaspoonful = *cucharadita, una*
technology = *tecnología, la*
telephone = *teléfono, el*
telephone, to = *telefonear*
telephonic = *telefónico*
television = *televisión, la*
tell, to = *contar*
tell off, to = *regañar*
temperature = *temperatura, la*
temperature, to have a = *tener fiebre*
ten = *diez*
tennis = *tenis, el*
tenth = *décimo*
thank goodness! = *¡menos mal!*
thank you (very much) = *(muchas) gracias*
that (after a verb) = *que*

that, those (demonstrative adjective) = *ese, esa, esos, esas*
that, those (demonstrative pronoun) = *ése, ésa, ésos, ésas*
that is to say, i.e. = *es decir*
that said = *dicho esto*
that which = *el que*
that's right = *eso es*
the (masculine singular) = *el, la, los, las*
theatre = *teatro, el*
their = *su(s)*
them (direct object pronoun) = *los*
them, to them = *les*
themselves = *se*
then = *luego*
then, so then = *entonces*
there (in the distance) = *allá;* (quite near) *allí*
there is, there are = *hay*
there wasn't/there weren't = *no había*
therefore = *por lo tanto*
thermometer = *termómetro, el*
they = *ellos/as*
thief = *ladrón, el*
thin = *delgado*
thing = *cosa, la*
think, to = *pensar (ie)*
think, believe, to = *creer*
think that, to = *opinar que*
third = *tercero*
thirty = *treinta*
this = *éste/a/o*
thousand = *mil*
three = *tres*
three hundred = *trescientos*
through = *por*
Thursday = *jueves*
ticket = *entrada, la*
tights, stockings = *medias, las*
time = *hora, la; tiempo, el*
time (occasion) = *vez, la* (pl.: *veces*)
timetable = *horario, el*
timid = *tímido*
tired = *cansado*
tired, to be = *tener sueño*
title = *título, el*
to = *a*
toast = *tostada, la*
toasted = *tostado*
toaster = *tostador, el*
today = *hoy*
together = *juntos*

tolerate, to = *aguantar; soportar*
tomato = *tomate, el*
tomorrow = *mañana*
tonic = *tónica, la*
too (also) = *también*
too (too much) = *demasiado*
tooth = *diente, el*
top = *máximo*
tortoise = *tortuga, la*
tourism = *turismo, el*
tourist = *turista, el/la*
tourist information office = *oficina de turismo, la*
town, village = *pueblo, el; pueblecito, el*
town hall = *ayuntamiento, el*
tracksuit = *chándal, el*
tradition = *tradición, la*
traffic-light = *semáforo, el*
trainers = *zapatillas (de deporte), las*
translate, to = *traducir*
travel, to = *viajar*
travel agents = *agencia de viajes, la*
tree = *árbol, el*
trendy = *de moda*
tropical = *tropical*
trouble = *pena, la*
trousers, pair of = *pantalón, el*
true = *verdadero*
truth = *verdad, la*
try (attempt), to = *intentar*
try, sample, to = *probar (ue)*
try, to = *procurar*
try on, to = *probarse (ue)*
try to, to = *tratar de*
t-shirt = *camiseta, la*
Tuesday = *martes*
tuna = *atún, el*
turkey = *pavo, el*
turn, to = *doblar; torcer*
tutorial = *tutoría, la*
tv (television) = *tele, la*
twelve = *doce*
twenty = *veinte*
twin = *gemela, la*
two = *dos*
two hundred = *doscientos*
type = *tipo, el*
typical = *típico*
ugly = *feo*
umbrella = *paraguas, el*
uncle = *tío, el*
under = *debajo de*

underline, to = *subrayar*
understand, to = *comprender*
uniform = *uniforme, el*
university = *universidad, la*
unjust = *injusto*
unkind = *antipático*
until = *hasta*
upstairs = *arriba*
Uruguay = *Uruguay, el*
us, to us = *nos*
USA = *Estados Unidos, los*
use, to = *utilizar*
useful = *útil*
valid = *válido (val.)*
varied = *variado*
various = *vario*
vegetables = *verduras, las; hortalizas, las*
vegetarian = *vegetariano*
Venezuela = *Venezuela* (fem.)
verb = *verbo, el*
very = *muy*
very much = *muchísimo*
video = *vídeo, el*
villa = *chalet, el*
village = *pueblo, el*
vinegar = *vinagre, el*
virgo (star sign) = *virgo*
virus = *virus, el*
visit, to = *visitar*
vital = *superimportante*
volley-ball = *voleibol, el*
waiter, waitress = *camarero/a, el/la*
wake up, to = *despertarse (ie)*
Wales = *Gales* (masc.)
wall (of a building) = *pared, la*
want, to = *querer (ie)*
want to, to = *tener ganas de*
wardrobe, cupboard = *armario, el*
wash, to (trans.) = *lavar*
wash oneself, to = *lavarse*
washing-machine = *lavadora, la*
watch = *reloj, el*
watch, to = *mirar*
water = *agua, el* (fem.)
water sports = *deportes acuáticos, los*
water-skiing = *esquí aquático, el*
way = *vía, la*
we = *nosotros/as*
wear, to = *llevar*
weather = *tiempo, el*
weather forecast = *pronóstico del tiempo, el*

Wednesday = *miércoles*
week = *semana, la*
weekend = *fin de semana, el*
weigh, to = *pesar*
weight = *peso, el*
well = *bien*
Welsh = *galés*
west = *oeste, el*
what? = *¿qué?*
what? (interrog.) = *¿cuál?*
what a pain! = *¡qué pesado!*
what a pain! = *¡qué rollo!*
what a shame! = *¡qué lástima!*
what a shame! = *¡qué pena!*
what a shame! = *¡vaya!*
what are....like? = *¿cómo son?*
what do you think about it? = *¿qué te parece?*
what is....like? = *¿cómo es?*
what is your name? (formal) = *¿cómo se llama usted?*
what is your name? (informal) = *¿cómo te llamas?*
whatever you want = *lo que quieras*
when = *cuándo*
when? (interrog.) = *¿cuándo?*
where = *donde*
where? = *¿dónde?*
where on earth have you been? = *¿dónde demonios has estado?*
where there's a will, there's a way = *querer es poder*
where to? = *¿adónde?*
which? = *¿cuál?*
while = *mientras que*
whisk, to = *batir*
white = *blanco*
whiteboard = *pizarra, la*
who (relative pronoun) = *quien*
who? = *¿quién?*
why? = *¿por qué?*
wife = *mujer, la*

wind = *viento, el*
window = *ventana, la*
windsurfing = *windsurfing, el*
windy, it's = *hace viento*
wine = *vino, el*
winter = *invierno, el*
wish = *gana, la*
with = *con*
with best wishes = *un abrazo*
with you = *contigo*
witness = *testigo, el*
woman = *mujer, la*
word = *palabra, la*
work = *trabajo, el*
work, to = *trabajar; funcionar*
working (adj.) = *laboral*
world = *mundo, el*
world, of the (adj) = *mundial*
worry (about), to = *preocuparse (por)*
worst thing, the = *lo peor*
worth, to be = *valer*
worthwhile, to be = *merecer la pena*
write, to = *escribir*
year = *año, el;* (school) *curso, el*
yell, to = *gritar*
yellow = *amarillo*
yes = *sí*
yesterday = *ayer*
yet = *todavía*
yoghurt = *yogur, el*
you = *tú; vosotros/as;* (polite) *usted (vd.), ustedes (vds.)*
young = *joven*
younger = *menor*
your (of you singular) = *tu(s)*
your (of you plural) = *vuestro*
yourself = *te*
yourselves = *os*
zone, area = *zona, la*
zoo = *zoo, el*